PIAZZA ARMERINA

THE ROMAN VILLA OF CASALE

MORGANTINA

EDIZIONI AFFINITÀ ELETTIVE

PIAZZA ARMERINA
THE ROMAN VILLA OF CASALE
MORGANTINA

Love for this land is the common factor that binds all those who have contributed to the creation of this work. Many thanks to Rosaria Falcone, Vincenzo Giusto, Gina Gulisano, Raimondo Marino, Elio Miccichè, Onofrio Prestifilippo, Carmen Scalisi and Sebastiano Tusa.
We would particularly like to thank Francesco Santalucia, Salvatore Generoso, Antonio Di Seri, the Regional Tourist Office, the Municipality of Piazza Armerina, G Media Publishers and the Regional Archaeological Museum of the Imperial Villa of Casale.

Dedicated to Federica and Tiziana

PHOTOGRAPHS AND ILLUSTRATIONS

Salvatore Centorrino: pages 132, 134, 135, 138, 139.
Alfio Garozzo: pages 3, 7, 9, 11, 13, 22, 23, 26, 27, 28, 29, 30, 32, 34, 35, 36, 38, 39, 40, 41, 42, 43, 45, 47, 48, 52, 53, 55, 56, 59, 62, 64, 65, 66, 67, 68, 71, 79, 87, 133, 136, 139.
Ettore Guccio: page 6.
Walter Leonardi: pages 4, 10, 16, 26, 36, 37, 40, 45, 46, 48, 49, 51, 54, 58, 59, 63, 71, 73, 76, 78, 80, 81, 98, 133, 135.
Riccardo Lombardo: page 142.
Raimondo Marino: pages 5, 21, 41, 54, 60, 61, 70, 81, 82, 86, 87, 88, 89, 90, 92, 93, 94, 95, 96, 97, 100, 101, 102, 103, 104, 105, 106, 107, 108, 109, 110, 111, 112, 113, 114, 116, 117, 118, 119, 120, 121, 122, 123, 124, 125, 126, 127, 136.
Melo Minnella: pages 128, 129, 141, 143.
Alessandro Saffo: pages 21, 50, 54.
Antonio Zimbone: pages 38, 46, 49, 50, 60, 61, 69, 75, 78, 85, 86, 107, 108.

Cover photographs: Front **Alfio Garozzo**, Back **Marino, Leonardi, Garozzo, Leonardi.**

GRAPHIC DESIGN: Claudio Falino
DRAWINGS AND PLAN OF THE VILLA: Donatella Di Marco

TRANSLATIONS
French: Bernard Michaud - English: Nicholas Whithorn
Spanish: Maria Teresa Monterisi - German: Doreen Lamek

Printed in June 2003
by Avvenire 2000 via Area Artigianale, agglomerato ASI
98129 Larderia Inferiore - Messina

Welcome

It is a beautiful day. In the Circus Maximus in Rome the Emperor is watching a chariot race. A short distance away, your attention is drawn by a group of athletes running with shields in their hands. Oblivious of all the eyes gazing at her, a woman undresses with the help of her servants.

If you can see all these scenes you are not dreaming, it must mean that you are visiting the lovely Villa del Casale, one of the most important and best preserved Roman monuments in the world, declared a world heritage site by UNESCO.

Just three kilometres from the Villa, the town of Piazza Armerina has everything you need to bring you back to earth. It is the ideal place for a relaxing holiday with a touch of culture thrown in. It is a town in which there is a happy compromise between the natural and manmade environment. During the hot summer the climate is made cooler by the 20,000 hectares of luxuriant woodland surrounding the town, making it an ideal holiday location. It is also a historic town and, thanks to its numerous monuments, it is a centre of culture and art with a heritage worth discovering.

If you happen to come to Piazza Armerina in August you absolutely should not miss the "Palio dei Normanni", a charming festival of parades in period costumes.

Finally, you should not leave without having visited the archaeological site of Morgantina, one of the most important ancient cities in Sicily, which will give you the incredible feeling of travelling back in time.

The Roman Villa of Casale

Among the large country houses of the late Roman period, the Villa of Casale is perhaps the best preserved of those surviving. It is especially famous for the splendid mosaic floors that decorate almost all the rooms and is considered to be one of the most important Roman monuments in the world. It is composed of four groups of buildings on four different levels (following the slope of the hillside), set in peaceful green countryside at the foot of Monte Mangone, in the Gela river valley.

Its existence had been known of for some considerable time, but only in 1881 did digging begin and only since 1950 have there been serious efforts to uncover it systematically and to preserve it; the servants quarters still remain to be uncovered.

The building (2nd century AD), was originally a simple construction, but was enlarged and rebuilt at the end of the 3rd century so as to become a luxurious country house in the centre of a large estate. The estate was composed of a small village and several mansiones (farms) where slaves and procuratores (overseers) were engaged in cultivating the fertile land.

Nearby, there was a place used for as a stop-off point and market place called Philosophiana, on the road connecting Catania to Agrigento, mentioned in the "Itineraria Antoninii", a sort of tourist guide book of the 1st century AD.

The new owner of the Villa could have been a rich landowner, a Senator, or even the Emperor Maximianus himself, a man of humble origins

from Pannonia.

He became Emperor after having served in the Roman army as a General under Diocletian, who appointed him co-regent and gave him the name of Herculius (under the divine protection of Hercules).

He achieved numerous military victories, particularly in Gaul, and was Emperor from 286 to 305 AD. The richly decorated Villa could

date back to the age of Maximianus but some researchers date it later.

Stylistically the mosaics are similar to those in Tunisia and Algeria around 300 AD.

The mosaic designs, made of African stone help in the task of dating them: the hairstyles and beards of the figures were fashionable at that time; the cylindrical hats worn by state officials and military officers are of Illyrian type, popular at the time of Diocletian, and the stick with a mushroom shaped handle carried by some of the dignitaries comes from the tetrarchy period.

The capitals of the columns found in several rooms belong to a type mass produced at the time of Diocletian and were also used in the Palace in Split.

Throughout the Villa the common theme is that of Hercules, symbol of the reigning Emperor, according to a panegyric of 289 AD, offered by the Emperor Maximianus Herculius, who compared his victories to the labours of Hercules.

It is interesting to note that the Liber Pontificalis refers to Constantine's possessions in Sicily (around Catania) and it is possible that he inherited these lands from Maxentius, son of Maximianus, after having defeated him in 312.

Top: the polygonal courtyard and spa.

Facing page: aerial view of the Villa.

Bottom: Roman coin with effigy of Emperor Maximianus Herculius.

History of the Villa

The luxurious villa was built between the end of the 3rd and the beginning of the 4th century AD, at the centre of a rural settlement within a very large estate. The buildings, with a total of about 60 rooms, stand three kilometres outside Piazza Armerina.

According to Prof. Vinicio Gentile, the villa was the summer residence of the Roman Emperor Maximianus Herculeus, who had it built at the end of the 3rd century AD on the site of a previous 2nd century rustic villa. Not all the experts agree with this evaluation.

This was the period of the tetrarchy, when the Roman Empire was divided into two parts by Diocletian: an eastern part, with Byzantium as capital, and a western one, with Mediolanum as capital.

The tetrarchy (from the Greek, four joint rulers) was established in 293 in order to better administer the Roman Empire, which was undergoing incursions at that time from the west by Alemanni and Burgundians, in Africa by Mauritanians and from the east by Parthians.

In the west Maximianus was made Emperor with the title of Augustus and he nominated Flavius Constantius his coadjutor and successor. In the east Diocletian was Emperor and he nominated Galerius as his coadjutor.

During the Roman era this area was full of woodland and wild animals and the Gela river, which flowed nearby, supplied the villa complex with water by means of an aqueduct. There were also numerous other water sources which allowed the land to be intensively farmed.

The villa was occupied by the Romans until the year 440, when the Vandals and, later, the Visigoths and the Ostrogoths invaded Sicily in waves, plundering and destroying everything they could. In 535 Belisarius, a General of the Byzantine Emperor Justinian, succeeded in defeating the Barbarians and occupied Sicily. During this period the villa regained its ancient splendour: this has been revealed by restoration work undertaken in the "Greasing Room" and in the Frigidarium. The Byzantines occupied it for about three centuries until the Arabs invaded Sicily in 827 and founded a kingdom, with Palermo as its capital. During the Arab period the villa was inhabited and the surrounding land was intensively farmed. This area was known for centuries as the "Village of the Saracens". In 1060 Roger the Norman re-conquered Sicily for Christianity and his descendants reigned until 1194. The arrival of the Normans brought about the rebirth of the villa.

After a long period of abandonment a very large landslide on Monte Mangone completely buried the villa, leaving it hidden for seven centuries. It is thanks to this mountain, then, that this beautiful villa has remained almost intact until the present day.

According to Prof. Gentili, the villa was called "Palatia" in Roman times. Later on, the Normans built a village near the villa and called it Platia. The village was destroyed by William the Bad in 1161 because it had given shelter to the Barons who had rebelled against him. In 1163 William gave permission for another town to be built, first called Platia and then Piazza. The word Armerina was added in 1862, after the unification of Italy.

The mosaics decorating this villa can be considered one of the wonders of the ancient world: in 1997 UNESCO declared the villa a "World Heritage Site", placing it under protection.

The Discovery of the Villa

The first documentary evidence of the existence of this beautiful dates back to 1640, when the first "History of Piazza" by the famous historian G.P. Chiarandà was published. On page 7 it says: "At the foot of a high mountain, called Mangone (an Arabic name meaning fortress) the ruins of a house can be seen, a house without an official name: the locals call it "Casale dé Saracini" (Villa of the Saracens)".

From that moment on, up to the end of the 19th century, the area was visited by numerous unofficial 'diggers' and a lot of artefacts were stolen. It was only in 1881 that the town council of Piazza Armerina entrusted restoration work to the engineer Pappalardo, who uncovered the floor of the Triclinium with the portrayal of the "Labours of Hercules". The work was completed by Senator Paolo Orsi in 1929. In 1939-40 Cultrera began digging in the "Large Hunting Ambulacrum", but it was only from the 1950s onwards (under

the supervision of the Siracusa Superintendence directed by Luigi Bernabò Brea) that complete scientific excavations were undertaken. This complex operation was conducted by Prof. Vinicio Gentile, assisted by Vittorio Veneziano and by two local experts, Di Seri and Anzaldi, who bear living testimony of the work undertaken. After ten years of excavations, the whole of the noble family's part of the villa was brought to light, along with its splendid mosaics. However, much of the complex remains to be discovered: an aerial photograph of 1960 shows an entire village lying under the ground to the south of the main entrance. There are probably storehouses, stables and accommodation for foremen, servants and slaves. Recently, several outhouses, a furnace and a small aqueduct have been uncovered. Several Byzantine tombs have been found on the hill above the villa.

In 1970 the architect Minissi designed the plexiglass shelters to protect the mosaics from the elements. The villa is open to visitors, who view the rooms of the villa from raised walkways.

The Mosaics

The mosaics cover a floor area of about 3,500 m² in almost all the rooms of the villa. They can be considered the most extensive and most beautiful Roman mosaics in existence. The technique of mosaics, which the Romans learnt from the Greeks, consists of creating pictures with tesserae about 1 cm in size. The artisans who created these magnificent floors were North Africans from Tunisia,

Bottom: restoration work.

where similar mosaics have been discovered.

In the villa the artists used two different types of tesserae: all the figures of people and animals were made with very small tesserae ("opus verniculatum"), while the geometric patterns were made using slightly larger tesserae ("opus tesselatum"). The only exception is the floor of the Basilica, which is covered with small pieces of high quality marble ("opus sectile"). As many as 37 different colours were used in the mosaics of the villa; of these, 21 are natural colours (marble and stone tesserae) and 16 are glass tesserae. All the walls of the villa are made of local sandstone ("opus incerta") and some of them still bear marvellous frescoes. The bricks used in the building, both square and rectangular, are made of baked clay ("opus latericium").

Onofrio Prestifilippo

The two faces of landownership: The Villa of Casale and Sophiana

A document dating back to the early Middle Ages was found among the yellowed papers of a family archive. It is unique written evidence of a long oral tradition, dating back to the 6th century, in which a certain Lucio Valerio recorded the words of one of his ancestors, who had been a witness to the arrival of the Vandals in Sicily, speaking about the Roman Villa of Casale. This written document had notes made in the margin in the early 1900s. the following story is based on this document. For the sake of clarity, any additions made are shown in italics.

The residence was situated down there, in the far off land of Sicily, and it was known among the high Roman aristocracy as the "Imperial Villa of Casale" because of the grandeur of the buildings and the refined beauty of the mosaics, which could rival those in the Emperor's own residence. Until just a few decades before it was built by one of our ancestors, nobody would have bet on the future of the Island. In the words of Martialis, it existed but was worth nothing and the very mention of its name was enough to turn people's blood cold. Since it was too eccentric to play an active part in politics, Sicily was considered suitable for housing inconvenient exiles and those who could cause trouble to the Empire. In 309, following riots that broke out in Rome, Emperor Maxentius exiled Pope Eusebius there, where he died in misery and poverty.

Its lack of political importance did not prevent our family and others among the most important in Rome and the Emperor himself from owning extensive estates where considerable quantities of wheat were grown and then transported to the port of Ostia, from where it was distributed to the population of Rome. The regular supply of the "annona", as distribution of this precious food source was called, served as a calming element in order to prevent further disorders among an urban population that was by nature compliant.

Our Emperors had paid particular attention to the supply of this precious cereal, which had been brought to Rome from the furthest corners of the Empire.

In a mosaic found in Ostia, the personification of Sicily appears next to those of Spain, Africa and Egypt, the four most famous wheat growing provinces of the Roman Empire. On a 3rd century base in the Vatican Museums, it is flanked by the figure of the goddess Annona.

The Casale Villa would have remained an unrealised dream but for an extremely important political event that decided the destiny of the Empire and, consequently, that of Sicily and of our family. I refer to the transfer of the capital to Constantinople, which took place in

332AD. The birth of the "new Rome" altered the balance that had governed the supply of grain for centuries. From that moment on the grain reserves of Egypt were destined for the new capital, leaving Rome short of supplies.

From then on the African grain supply became essential for the future of millions of Romans and Sicily acquired a strategic role of fundamental importance.

The Island had not seen military activity since the era of the Roman conquest but now it was the base for military expeditions sent to discourage any signs of revolt in Africa; supplies of grain crossed the Island on their way to the capital; the Island supplied extra cereals when there were famines, raids by Barbarians or resistance from functionaries in Africa. The Island became the focal point for the interests of our family and numerous other aristocratic families. Sicily became a stop off on the inspection trips to the far off African territories and political positions were much sought after as a step in the direction of obtaining a vicariate or a proconsulship in Africa. The port of Agrigento overflowed with marble arriving from Phocaea, destined to be used in the construction of villas belonging to the most important members of the Roman nobility, from the Aurelii to the Simmachi from the Nicomachi to the Valerii, for use as a base during holidays or periods of work.

For their holidays they used a special guide called "Itinerarium per maritima loca". Unlike the other map, "Itinerarium Antonini", which showed the glorious Greek cities of the past or the villas on the estates, the former concentrated on the coast road between Agrigento and Syracuse, showing sanctuaries and spas on the map.

The Thermae Selinuntinae (Selinunte Spa), the most famous spa in the ancient world, is still open for business on Mount San Calogero in Sciacca. I refer, of course, to a very exclusive kind of tourism, limited to Senators, as we were the only ones with the necessary time,

money and, above all, the privilege of being able to travel freely on the public highways of the province.

This was excessive presumption on our part and the Emperors often tried to restrain us, worried about the efficiency of the "cursus pubblicus" (public highway), which was reserved for use by the postal service and for the transportation of goods.

Four centuries after the Romans had built the military roads all along the coast from Messina to the port of Lilibeum (modern day Marsala), natural point of passage towards Africa, changes were made to the road system. We Senators, the landowners of central southern Sicily, who had ensured that the road network provided a link between the cities of Catania and Agrigento, as well as the numerous villas belonging to the landowners.

The Casale Villa was slightly inland of the new road that crossed its possessions and led to the ancient town of Sophiana, a few miles further on. There we had established a stop off point for travellers where they could find accommodation for the night and change horses. Sophiana was also a marketplace for our produce and a postal station, also used for tax collection.

The settlement of Sophiana, which covers an area of about eight hectares to the south of the provincial road to Mazzarino, flourished from the early imperial age until the year 250AD, when it was razed to the ground. In the age of Constantine the large estate, covering 1,500 hectares, passed into the possession of a member of the Roman aristocracy and Senate who had decided to live in Sicily because of political and landowning interests. The Casale Villa was probably the "pars dominica" (manor house) of this estate. Archaeological digs have brought to light the manor house, a spa, and several very large commercial and residential buildings.

Our ancestors loved living off their riches and preferred to spend their wealth rather than increase it, so much so that the wealth and income of our family remained practically at the same level, from the era of Augustus up to the time of the Barbarian invasion. We were exploiters, we have to admit it, we had our pockets full of gold and then we wasted it. If we had adopted the cradle plough, instead of using crude primitive tools, we would have been able to plough deeper and we would have been repaid with more abundant harvests. If we had used reaping and threshing machines, we would have had fewer labourers to feed. If we had introduced the watermill, we would have been better prepared to face periods of drought. We were not so astute as those who successfully used these new technologies in the same period in Gaul and in Lombardy. *These and other ingenious tools were introduced in Sicily four centuries later by the Arabs.*

Latin was spoken at the Casale, but only in the family circle. In order to be understood by the locals it was necessary to speak in Greek. The survival of the Greek language in the numerous small towns and villages scattered around us made us feel like foreigners in a land that we had usurped. You had to visit the coastal towns in order to hear our language spoken. In these towns Latin was gradually catching on and pushing out Greek, which started to become a rural language, spoken in areas like the Casale or nearby Sophiana.

Our Villa was surrounded by luxuriant greenery, thanks to the waters of the Gela river. The hills which lined the river banks were covered with evergreen trees that hid a wide variety of animals, perfect for more or less serious hunting parties. In the shade of these leafy branches our ancestors enriched their spirit, dedicating themselves to study, philosophy and contemplation, while they restored their bodies with swimming, bathing and hunting.

From high up on the hills the view took in the never-ending bare land of the estate, the undisputed kingdom of golden wheat covering every inch of the gently sloping hillside. The changing colours of the seasons were like those of an artist's palette, from the still green of winter to the marbled green of spring, from the golden yellow of ripe corn to the to the straw colour of summer. The hills were a succession of Mediterranean scrub, oak woods and clearings. Sheep, goats, horses and cattle all found plenty to feed on. The rich grazing land fattened the sheep and made their wool grow long and thick. In the oak woods black pigs wandered around searching for acorns which added fat to their loins. Horses became agile and fast while the cattle grazed happily in the grassy clearings, blissfully unaware of the fact that they would be castrated once they reached the age of three. Most of the land was given over to farming by families tied to the land. The use of servants was limited to the *pars dominica*, which was still directly managed by our ancestors or their trustees. Centuries-old olive trees, said to have been planted by the Greeks, grew on the land. The "liquid gold", as Homer called it, competed with African grain on the tables in Rome. Green pomegranate trees with their scarlet fruit brought to mind Proserpine and her sin of gluttony, when she ate the red pips and was condemned to spend six months of each year in the infernal regions. The production of honey was the real feather in the cap for the estate, because of the abundance of sweet-smelling essences that covered the surrounding hillsides. The bee-hives, made of ferula wood and clay were lined up under canopies. All in all, our Villa was an efficient productive unit which provided a lucrative supply of produce for export, sold at the nearby market in Sophiana. We produced everything that Rome required from Sicily, with the exception of sulphur, pitch and rock salt. The latter product was transported along the "cursus pubblicus" between Agrigento and Catania so frequently that it became known as the 'salt road'.

Elio Miccichè

15

Visiting the Villa

Following the avenue leading to the Villa, on the left you will see the arched Roman aqueduct, 50 metres long, which carried water from the Gela river to the spa and the fountains.

A secondary aqueduct is situated behind the private latrine and served the other part of the Villa.

Continuing along the avenue you arrive at the first of the four levels on which the Villa is built.

This level is a spa complex, including pools, a gymnasium and a sauna, equipped with a heating system that allowed hot air to circulate under the floor and in the cavities between the brickwork of the walls.

The spa in the Villa is a small scale reproduction of those which graced every Roman town and were widely used both in Rome and in every province of the Empire.

Let's begin our visit with the Praefurnia, Calidaria, Tepidarium and Frigidarium.

Bottom: avenue leading to the Villa.

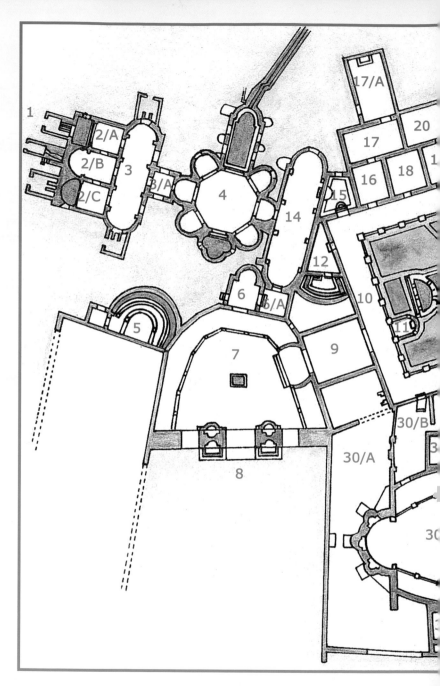

1 Praefurnia – Ovens for heating the water and air of the spa complex
2/A Male Calidarium; 2/B Sauna; 2/C Female Calidarium
3 Tepidarium
3/A Room for greasing and massage after bathing.
4 Frigidarium – Seascapes in the centre and bathing scenes in some of the

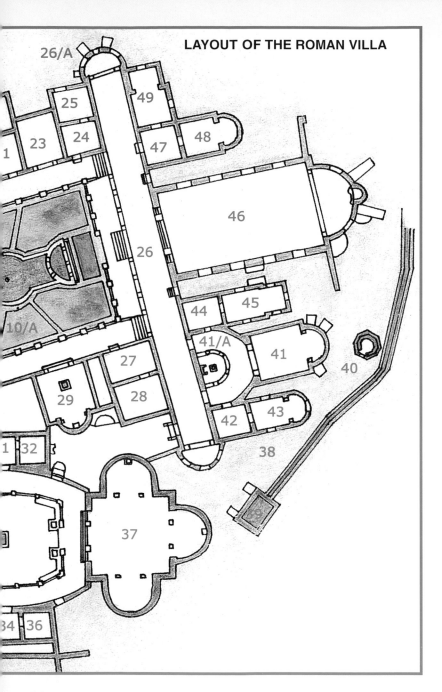

LAYOUT OF THE ROMAN VILLA

niches
5 Large latrine
6 Shrine of Venus
6/A Spa Vestibule for servants
7 Polygonal courtyard with Ionic columns

8 Ancient entrance to the Villa, originally with 3 arches
9 Adventus Vestibule – Guests were greeted in this room
10 Peristyle – Rectangular four-sided portico with 32 columns
10/A Garden containing large pond with statue of Cupid
11 Votive shrine for worship of the Lares who protected Roman households
12 Courtyard
13 Latrine with mosaics depicting running wild animals
14 Large gymnasium – The mosaics depict chariot races in the Circus Maximus
15 Trapezoidal Vestibule – The mosaics probably depict Eutropia, Maximianus' wife and mistress of the Villa, with her children
16 Arab or Norman furnace room
17 Servants' room with geometrical mosaics
17/A Kitchen with basin
18 Room with star patterned mosaic
19 Rectangular room without mosaics
20 Bedroom with dance or theatre inspired decorations
21 Four seasons room
22 Fishing cupids room
23 Small Hunting Room – Hunters making a sacrifice to Diana
24 Servants' room with octagonal patterned mosaic
25 Servants' bedroom. Square patterned mosaics
26 Large Hunting Ambulacrum or corridor (60 metres long)
26/A On the left: apse with mosaics depicting Mauritania (Africa)
26/B On the right: apse with mosaics showing scenes from India or Armenia
27 Servants' room with geometrical patterned mosaic
28 Room depicting ten girls in "bikinis" doing gymnastics
29 Diaeta of Orpheus – Rectangular room for listening to music
30 Xystus – Wide open-air atrium in an ellipsoid shape
30/A Triclinium kitchen
30/B Corridor linking the four-sided portico with the Xystus
31 Putti pressing grapes; 32 Cupids harvesting grapes; 33 Vine growing; 34 Cupids fishing; 35 Eroti fishing; 36 Seafaring putti
37 Triclinium – Large dining-hall with apses on three sides
38 Secondary aqueduct
39 Castellum Aquae (water collection tank)
40 Octagonal latrine for members of the family
41 Diaeta of Arion – The mistress's sitting-room
41/A Atrium with semicircular portico with Ionic columns and central impluvium
42 Vestibule of the small circus – mosaics of chariots driven by children
43 Bedroom (cubicle) used by the mistress's daughter
44 Vestibule of Eros and Pan – The mosaic shows Eros and Pan wrestling
45 Bedroom used by one of the children of the owner of the Villa. In the ante-room mosaics with children hunting
46 Basilica – Large hall for official functions
47 Vestibule of Polyphemus – Large mosaic portraying Ulysses and Polyphemus
48 Fruit cubicle – Bedroom used by the mistress (domina) of the Villa. The mosaics in the ante-room depict laurel wreaths with fruit
49 Bedroom used by the owner of the Villa. Mosaic with erotic scenes

PRAEFURNIA (1)

To the left of the entrance avenue are the remains of three ovens, called Praefurnia (oven mouths), used for heating the air.

Originally there was a water tank situated on the central oven and the water from here passed into the Calidaria (2) and the Tepidarium (3), after being heated by the oven, through clay and lead pipes (fistulae). Hot air was circulated through the cavities under the floors, which rested on brick supports in order to allow this to happen. The floors used to become so hot that footwear was necessary. You can still see that the outside walls of the ovens were covered with terracotta pipes to avoid the loss of heat.

Top: base for the hot water pool.

CALIDARIA (2)

There are three rooms adjacent to the ovens and which were heated by them. These are not open to visitors and can only be viewed from the outside. The two rooms to either side contained the pools for hot water baths. The pool in the room on the right (2a) is very well preserved; on the walls you can see the tubules, through which the hot air circulated and which isolated the pool from the exterior walls and kept the water hot; the bottom of the pool is made of lead, covered with slabs of marble. A few steps gave access to the pool for the members of the family. This pool was probably for the men and the semi-circular one, in the room on the left (2c), was for the women. The central room (2b) was occupied by the sauna (laconicum) and had floors resting on bricks, in order to allow the hot air to circulate, and double walls with tubules. The temperature was controlled by windows situated high up and which were opened when the temperature rose too much. There was also a fountain for cold ablutions (labrum).

Bottom: clay pipes which carried hot air into the Spa.

21

Relaxation and Health

Roman spas were generally divided into two sections: male and female, with separate entrances. They were laid out according to a strict set of rules established by Vitruvius Pollio, a famous architect of the Augustan period, included in his massive ten volume work on the principles of art and the science of architecture. People undressed in the changing-room (apodyterium) and then moved on into the gymnasium, where they did exercises in order to warm up their bodies.

They then went into the calidarium, where there were always several pools for bathing in hot water, a labrum, a pool of cold water for cooling off, and a sauna (laconicum). The positioning of the laconica next to the tepidarium allowed people to bathe in warm water after sweating. After soaking in the tepidarium, which was heated by hot coals in the 1st and 2nd centuries and later by a hypocaustum heating system (hot air chamber), people then moved into the frigidarium, used for cold baths. People using the spa could, however, choose different routes, according to their personal preferences or the therapeutic vogues of the period.

Spas hosted numerous different activities: next to the bathing areas were others used for massage, with the use of oils rubbed into the skin to protect it from the sudden changes of temperature, before and after the calidarium, areas for depilation and for gymnastics. In some spas there were also rooms used for hosting conferences and public readings (auditoria), or even libraries.

The way in which Roman spas worked gives us an insight into very

interesting plumbing and building techniques. The heating system allowed for the passage of hot air under the floors, which were raised up on supports made of terracotta bricks (suspensurae), as well as in the cavities between the walls, lined with tiles (tegulae mammatae) or pipes. In adjacent areas there were ovens which heated the water.

The use of spas had a very important social role to play, as a meeting place, and shows, moreover, the great importance that the Romans placed on looking after their bodies.

Spas according to Lucius Annaeus

In order to get an idea of just what Roman spas were like in reality, we can turn to an authoritative source from that period: Lucius Annaeus.

In a letter he laid down the rules to be followed in order to make the spa a sacred place, explaining that the patrons would not have enjoyed their baths ".... if there were no large circular mirrors on the walls; if the Alexandrian marble were not combined with incrustations of Numidian marble; if this marble were not decorated with artistic mosaics; if the ceiling were not made of glass; if the marble from the Greek island of Thasos, which once could be found only in temples, did not surround the pools in which we lay our tired sweating bodies; if the water did not flow out of taps made of silver".

THE SPA OF THE ROMAN VILLA

TEPIDARIUM (3)

You can look into this long room with two apses through a window placed high up. This room was

used by patrons to cool off after using the hot baths and sauna. Also here you can see the raised floor used to allow the circulation of hot air coming from the ovens outside.

The mosaic in this room is, unfortunately, one of the few in the house that has almost completely been destroyed. It used to depict running athletes carrying shields in their left hands and torches in their right hands (lampadedromia, torchlight race). Stone pillars supported the ceiling, which was probably made of glass.

GREASING ROOM (3/A)

This is a very small room connecting the Frigidarium and the Tepidarium and may have been used for greasing and massage with oils after bathing.

The mosaics portray a young athlete (maybe the master of the house) being massaged by a slave; on the right, another slave is holding a flask of oil and a strigil, a curved tool used to cleanse the skin from sweat and oil; low down two slaves wearing loincloths are depicted, identified with the names of Titus and Cassius, one of whom has a conical hat showing that he is from Syria.

This room was probably restored sometime after the construction of the Villa.

Top: greasing room.

Bottom: large octagonal hall of the Frigidarium.

FRIGIDARIUM (4)

Continuing your visit you come into the Frigidarium.

This large octagonal room was used for cold baths and its peculiar architecture is similar to that of the octagonal hall in Nero's Domus Aurea and is certainly a predecessor of polygonal buildings of the Christian period, such as the Baptistery in Albenga and San Vitale in Ravenna.

The central mosaic shows a seascape with cupids fishing, Nereides, Tritons, Centaurs and sea monsters: a recurring theme in African mosaics.

Only two of the mosaics in the surrounding niches are in good condition; one depicts a woman undressing with the help of two servants, and the other, to the right of the pool, shows a man sitting on a leopard skin stool attended by two servants handing him clothes.

In the two walls opposite the en-

On these pages, the attractive mosaics decorating the Frigidarium.

trances there are six large niches, one step up from the floor, which were used as changing-rooms (apodyterium).

They once contained benches on which clothes and towels could be laid.

On either side of these niches there are two pools: the one used for swimming is rectangular in shape and covered with marble slabs and was connected to the aqueduct by a small canal; the one used for cool bathing is trefoil in shape and had lead pipes in which the water was heated by the hot air circulating under the floor.

Columns with Corinthian capitals to the sides of the niches supported a domed ceiling made of blue glass and covered with mosaics.

Having concluded your visit to the spa, you move on to the second level, before entering the Villa proper, and here you will find the Large latrine (5), the Shrine of Venus (6), the Polygonal courtyard (7) and the original three-sided entrance to the Villa (8).

LARGE LATRINE (5)

This is opposite the spa complex and was reached through a small doorway.

The central part was open-air and the semi-circular part, which housed the seats, was sheltered by a

canopy supported by columns.
The water ran through a small canal, which can still be seen. The marble seats with a hole in the centre were situated directly above the canal (or sewer). A reconstruction of these can be seen in the small latrine.

SHRINE OF VENUS (6)

A small quadrangular room used as an entrance to the spa complex for servants.

The name of the room comes from the statue of Venus that was probably situated in the apse and some fragments of which have been found.

The mosaics have geometrical patterns, with four-petalled flowers and lilies.

From this room you can see the Vestibule of the spa (6/A), which led into the gymnasium.

This was used by servants and so has geometrical patterned mosaics, as is the case in all the rooms used by servants, and in this case they are particularly elaborate.

A double-ended plait joins up ellipses containing wave patterns.

On the walls traces of a fresco can still be seen. From the Shrine of Venus you go down a few steps into the polygonal courtyard.

POLYGONAL COURTYARD (7)

It is a spacious courtyard, surrounded by eleven columns with Ionic style capitals, once the atrium (entrance hall) of the Villa.

Guests waiting to be greeted once sat on the stone bench to the right of the entrance, under a canopy supported by columns.

The portico had a floor decorated with a colourful geometrical scaled pattern mosaic, traces of which can still be seen.

In the centre of the courtyard are the remains of the base of a fountain and a square pool used to collect rainwater (impluvium).

Facing page: reconstruction of the majestic three-arched entrance to the Villa.

Bottom: colonnade in the polygonal courtyard.

ENTRANCE TO THE VILLA (8)

Visitors in the 3rd century AD would certainly have been impressed by the majesty of the entrance hall: three wide arches gave access to the Villa. It takes a little imagination to be able to picture the magnificent entrance when all you can see now are the remains of the four pillars on which the arches stood and the two huge blocks of stone in front of the columns which were also part of the structure.

The central entrance arch was 4.5 metres wide and those to the side measured 2.6 metres. Each arch was flanked by six columns (the ones on show are reconstructions). At the base of the central pillars, under niches that once contained statues, there are four ornamental fountains (nymphaea), two in a shell shape inside and two rectangular ones on the outside. These nymphaea were dedicated to minor female divinities who personified seas, rivers and mountains. The fountains were continually fed with water that fell from their upper section built on three arches. The exterior façade of the entrance was decorated with frescoes and traces of these can be seen on the pillar to

Top: monumental entrance; bottom: large Polygonal courtyard with columns.

Bottom: monumental entrance.

the right, on which there is the figure of a military standard (signum) with the heads of four of the Emperors of the tetrarchy on medallions, something which would seem to confirm that the Villa belonged to Emperor Maximianus. Having visited the entrance and the polygonal courtyard you climb a few steps to the adventus vestibule, on the third level of the Villa.

ADVENTUS VESTIBULE (TABLINIUM) (9)

This room gave access to the large colonnade of the Villa and it was here that guests were welcomed. The scene shown in the white and red frame of the mosaics is that of a ritual welcoming such as that given to an Emperor

Facing page: the Peristyle mosaics depicting 162 animal heads.

(adventus Augusti). A similar scene is portrayed on the arch dedicated to the Emperor Galerius in Salonika. In the lower part of the mosaic three young men, with leaves round their heads, are holding a message (diptych) for the master of the house (dominus). In the upper part you can see a bearded high ranking official, well dressed and holding a candelabrum, and two young men holding laurel branches.

All of the six people shown are looking towards the central part of the mosaic, which, unfortunately, has been lost or removed and probably depicted the Emperor.

Bottom: the garden with fountain.

The walls were decorated with frescoes of life-size figures. This can be deduced from the fragment of fresco to be seen just above floor level on the southern wall.

PERISTYLE (10)

Climbing a few steps from the Vestibule you come into the beautiful Peristyle: a wide rectangular four-sided portico surrounded by 32 columns with capitals in Corinthian style supporting roofs jutting out into the garden. The garden was once home to peacocks, pheasants and doves and is now full of trees and box-tree hedges. In the centre of the garden there is a large pond with a fountain and a statue of a "cupid", the classi-

cal personification of the God of love. The peristyle was adopted by wealthy Roman families in their houses and villas instead of the atrium after having been influenced by the Greeks. The garden was a place for people to relax in peaceful luxuriant surroundings, with fountains and birds, and at the same time it gave light to all the rooms facing the portico.

The mosaics on the floors of the four porticoes depict 162 animal and bird heads with laurel wreaths. A point of curiosity: in front of the lararium (11) you can see that these medallions were not only for decorative purposes but indicated two different routes to follow.

The first of these, to the left, where the animal heads are facing one another, was used by the dominus, members of his family and guests; the second, to the right (the heads face in the opposite direction), is believed to have been for visitors and servants.

Both routes ended up at the foot of the three stairways leading to the Large Hunting Ambulacrum (26). The stairways to the side were used for going up and the central one for going down.

VOTIVE CHAPEL FOR WORSHIP OF THE LARES (11)

This small room was situated in the garden, exactly opposite the adventus Vestibule, because the Lares (the deified souls of deceased family members) had the task of protecting the house from evil. The head of the family made offerings of incense, flowers and libations to the lares. In the apse, which was once flanked by two marble columns, there is a pedestal on which a statue rested. The geometrical mosaics on the floor depict an eight-pointed star against two squares with multi-coloured plaits. In the centre of the pattern there is an ivy leaf (symbol of Maximianus' family) set inside a laurel wreath.

Bottom: trapezoidal latrine with mosaic of running animals.

COURTYARD (12) AND LATRINE (13)

Following the route to the left, you soon come to an open-air courtyard (used to disperse bad smells), which was entered through the portico and which

served as an ante-room to the small latrine for use by guests. The latrine has a trapezoid shape, slightly apsidal, and to the left of the entrance you will see the concrete reconstruction of the toilets (the original ones were in marble). Under these is a canal through which water flowed continually, ending up in the nearby river Gela. To the right of the entrance you can see a basin which was either used to supply water to the canal or maybe for washing. The mosaic on the floor portrays five running animal figures: a partridge, a hare, a leopard, a great bustard and a wild ass. Originally, there was a door providing a measure of privacy and you can still see the holes left by the hinges.

GYMNASIUM OR CIRCUS ROOM (14)

Following the walkway you can observe the Large Gymnasium of the Villa from above. It is a rectangular room with an apse on either side.

The dominus and his family entered through the Vestibule (15) and servants came in through the room adjacent to the Aedicule of Venus.

The Romans used to do exercises to warm up their muscles before using the spa. Along the sides you will notice the remains of eight columns, raised up above floor level, which originally had Corinthian capitals and supported the vaulted ceiling of this large room.

The walls were covered by frescoes imitating slabs of marble.

The design decorating the floor depicted chariot races in the Circus Maximus in Rome, in honour of Ceres, goddess of harvests. It is a work of extraordinary detail and completeness and gives a realistic idea of the atmosphere of these races.

The arena was divided into two parts by a central spina at the end of which were the finishing posts, made up of three bronze columns.

From right to left you can see: a winged Nike on a column, a stand (phala) for privileged spectators, the obelisk of Augustus, the Magna Mater on a lion, the

castellum acquae and large pools of water, the ovaria (the instrument used to show the number of laps) and another phala. The eight competitors, two each representing the four teams, were distinguished by the colour of the smock worn by the aurigae (drivers of the chariots). The teams russata (red smock), veneta (blue), albata (white) and prasina (green) competed over a distance of seven laps in the Circus Maximus, a total of seven kilometres.

In the mosaics in the apse you can see portrayals of the temples dedicated to Jupiter, Roma and Hercules; a chariot driver dressing for the competition; the twelve gates of the "carceres" through which the chariots raced at full speed (the carceres are surmounted by the statues of the twelve divinities of Olympus and by the tetrastyle stand from which the race was started by the magistrate responsible for organising the games). On the left, in the second apse, you can see Titus' triumphal arch, flanked by the stands crowded with spectators and a boy distributing loaves of bread.

The various stages of the race are depicted very clearly: the chaotic and dangerous start to the race, a collision between two chariots, one of which is on the point of turning over, and finally the presentation of the victory palm by the race judge, while a man blows a long tuba to signal the end of the race. It is a particularly lively design, full of movement and dynamism; it is, moreover, very realistic because it exactly reproduces what the Emperor could see from the Imperial loggia of the Circus Maximus, situated on the Palatine side. Professor S. Settis has also observed that the Emperor's view in the Villa can be pinpointed to the trapezoidal vestibule, from where the dominus entered on his way to the spa.

These details seem to support the theory that the dominus was indeed the Emperor himself.

TRAPEZOIDAL VESTIBULE (15)

This elegant room was used by the dominus, his family and guests to pass from the Peristyle into the Gymnasium. It is a small trapezoidal shaped room with a bench, covered by slabs of limestone, situated at the base of the walls. People sat here awaiting their turn to enter the spa: it was, quite simply, a waiting room. There was also a door that led into the nearby Kitchen (17/a) and to the outside.

The walls of this room were richly decorated with frescoes. The mosaics probably depict Eutropia, wife of Maximianus and domina (mistress) of the Villa, while on her way to bathe with her young children. She is particularly elegantly dressed and is wearing earrings and a necklace.

Her hair is tied up in the "helmet" style that was fashionable during the tetrarchy period. The eyes of the boy on her right show the squint from which her son Maxentius suffered. To either side two servants are carrying a basket for the clothes (on the left) and a red shoulder bag and basket (on the right). Note the shadows of the figures in the mosaic, shown in the form of black stripes on their feet.

ARAB OR NORMAN FURNACE ROOM (16)

The next room you come to, on the left-hand side of the colonnade, is the first of the rooms (16/18) used by servants attending to the guests in the adjacent rooms.

This room was also used as a vestibule for an inner room.

The floor has mosaics with geometrical patterns.

A kiln for firing pottery was built to the right of the entrance in either the Arab or Norman period.

ROOM WITH GEOMETRICAL PATTERNS (17)

This room was for use by servants and connected with the Kitchen (17/A). It is a large room with geometrical patterned mosaics.

Flowers with six petals, four-leaf clovers and stars are framed by squares, hexagons and stars.

KITCHEN (17/A)

This room is nowadays open to the elements. It is believed to have been used as a kitchen for preparing guests' meals.

The crockery for the kitchen was possibly stored on a long bench or table situated on the right-hand side of the room. The floor has no mosaics; at the end of the room there are the remains of a large rectangular sink.

ROOM WITH STAR PATTERNED MOSAIC (18)

This room was also for use by serving staff and was reached through the portico of the Peristyle.

The mosaic on the floor has a geometrical pattern. The pattern is composed of two superimposed squares, creating eight-pointed stars, inside which you will see roses intertwined with colourful ribbons.

ROOM OF THE LOST MOSAIC (19)

This room connected the portico with the Dancing Room (20). It acted as an anteroom for the guests' bedroom. Only a few fragments of the mosaic remain, the rest of the decoration having been completely lost.

DANCING ROOM (20)

This was a rectangular room used as a cubicle (bedroom) for guests.

The walls were frescoed and you can still see the remains of the original plasterwork.

The mosaic on the floor was seriously damaged by the construction of a wall in mediaeval times. It portrays a girl swirling a red veil around her head and a young man lifting his dancing partner from the ground.

The meaning of this mosaic is not completely clear since many believe it is not the portrayal of a dance but rather the scene of the "Rape of the Sabines".

This is suggested by the

fact that the girl being lifted from the ground seems to be trying to resist by pushing the young man away with her hand.

ROOM OF THE FOUR SEASONS (21)

This room acts as a vestibule for an inner room. It is entered from the Peristyle and was used by guests.

The mosaic on the floor is well preserved and depicts hexagons forming seven-pointed stars. The medallions contain scenes representing the four seasons: spring, a bust of a woman wearing roses in her hair, summer, a young man crowned with ears of wheat, autumn, a female figure with bunches of grapes in her

hair, winter, a man with a cape over one shoulder and leaves on his head.

Next to these medallions representing the seasons there are others containing the figures of fish and birds.

ROOM OF THE FISHING CUPIDS (22)

This is a rectangular room the use of which is unknown.

Some experts believe it was a dining-room (triclinium).

The mosaic is in good condition and depicts four boats with cupids fishing and a sea full of fish.

The cupids in the two boats on the left are pulling in a net; in the upper right boat you can see one cupid

holding a trident while the others pull in a line; in the lower right boat one of the cupids is emptying a fish trap and the others are collecting the catch.

Note the lively colours of the boats and, high up, the depiction of a villa with a long colonnade in the background of the scene; on the walls there are traces of frescoes.

SMALL HUNTING ROOM (23)

You have now reached the Small Hunting Diaeta: this was a sitting-room for guests and the mosaic recounts a day of hunting near the Villa.

The beautiful mosaic shows five hunting scenes, from left to right. In the first one two servants are taking dogs out to the hunting grounds

In the second scene, in the centre, a sacrifice is being made to Diana, goddess of hunting, by burning incense.

Some researchers have claimed to recognise the person making the sacrifice to Diana as Flavius Constantius, coadjutor of Maximianus, and, behind him, his son Constantine, the future Emperor. The figure to the right could represent Maxentius, Maximianus' son. In the third scene you can see two men under a tree hunting with the help of falcons and, in the centre, some hunters banqueting under a red canopy strung between two oak trees. The hunters are being served by slaves.

On the right a soldier on horseback is about to strike a hare. Finally, in the last scene, you can see, from

left to right, some deer being chased into a net by men on horseback and a wounded boar attacking the hunters.

ROOM WITH OCTAGONAL PATTERN MOSAIC (24)

This quadrangular room was used by staff serving the nearby rooms occupied by the dominus. It is a vestibule for an inner room (25) and is entered from the Peristyle.

The geometrical design of the floor mosaic contains large octagons with concave sides containing eight-petalled flowers and other floral motifs.

ROOM WITH SQUARE PATTERN MOSAIC (25)

It is believed that this room was a bedroom used by staff serving the rooms occupied by the dominus situated on the other side of the Large Hunting Ambulacrum (26).

The floor has a mosaic with geometrical designs, in particular squares circumscribed by a plait and containing a flower.

Top: mosaic depicting a sacrifice being offered to the goddess Diana.

LARGE HUNTING AMBULACRUM (26)

In this room you can see the most beautiful mosaics of the whole complex.

It is called the "Large Hunting Ambulacrum" because

of the magnificent hunting scene represented here. The Ambulacrum served as access to the rooms used by the dominus (47/49), to the Basilica (46) and to the rooms occupied by the domina and the children (41/45) situated to the right of the Basilica.

The route taken by visitors gives you the chance to see the mosaic close up as you walk across a carpet. The room is basically a 65 metre long corridor, with an apse at either end, decorated by mosaics depicting the personifications of two Roman provinces.

The one to the left portrays Mauritania (or more probably Africa) and the one to the right, which is badly damaged, shows Armenia or India. In the middle of the

two seas separating these continents is Italy and the scene depicts prey being transported towards Italy from all over the Empire for the great public feasts in Rome.

The whole central part of the room is occupied by the hunting scene, which takes place in the African countryside, with buildings and colonnades, on a hillside near a river and the sea. Men carrying shields and long spears hunt various species of wild animals,

portrayed in their natural habitat. One man is being attacked by a lioness and his companion is trying to help him by spearing the animal. The scenes depict the capture of animals rather than their slaughter, indeed you can see a leopard enticed into a trap using a goat as bait, while the hunters wait hidden in the bushes. Another man is being chased by a tigress after having stolen her cubs and drops one of them in order to distract the mother's attention.

The captured animals are loaded onto ships to be transported to Rome and other cities for use in amphitheatres; some of them are locked in cages and transported on carts, while others are put on a lead like a dog. There is an Imperial official, perhaps Maximianus himself, in charge of the operations.

He is wearing a richly decorated cape and a cylindrical hat;

the man accompanying him has a sign with the letter H on his shoulder, perhaps to indicate that he belongs to the "Herculia" legion, thus named in honour of Maximianus.

In this highly realistic scene it is impossible to explain

why there should be a winged griffon clutching a cage containing a dead man. Some researchers believe that this scene is a symbol of the death of one of the hunters during the hunt, but the meaning is still not completely clear.

ROOM OF THE GIRLS IN "BIKINI" (28)

To the right of the Large Hunting Ambulacrum there are two rooms which were probably for use by ser-

vants who looked after the nearby rooms used by the domina. The first one (27) is a rectangular room, with frescoes on the wall and geometrical patterned mosaics.

The second (28), which was probably originally a room for servants, became a gymnasium for the daughters of the dominus. High up on the left you can

see a corner of the original floor mosaic, from the 3rd century, with a geometrical pattern. The present mosaic depicts ten girls doing gymnastics or taking part in some kind of race. The figure in a tunic is acting as a referee and is offering a crown to one of the winners.

The fact that one of the girls has a scar leads us to believe that the people depicted are members of the family and that the mosaic refers to an event that really took place.

The gymnasts are extremely modern looking, wearing subligar, the briefs of that time, and stropkion, a sort of top. In the upper part of the mosaic the athletes are engaged in the long jump with weights, in the discus and in running.

In the lower part, apart from the above mentioned referee, there are two winners and two other girls playing handball.

DIAETA OF ORPHEUS (29)

The next room is a large hall used for listening to music. It is rectangular in shape with an apse containing a statue of Apollo.

The entrance has two columns; in the centre of the room, in the floor mosaic, the mythological Orpheus is depicted in a frame of laurels playing the lyre while seated on a rock.

Around him birds and other animals, even large ones, are enchanted and bewitched by his music. The scene is very subtle and delicate. There was also a fountain in the room and you can still see the base.

After visiting the Diaeta of Orpheus, your route takes you back towards the Large Hunting Ambulacrum and the apse of India. From here you pass into a spacious courtyard, decorated with columns, which connected the family's quarters with the Ovoid Portico (30) and the Triclinium (37).

Top: the statue of Apollo in the Diaeta of Orpheus.

Bottom: the Ovoid Portico.

OVOID PORTICO OR XYSTUS (30)

Large colonnaded atrium in an elliptic shape situated in front of the Triclinium (37), where the guests dined. Brick pillars and marble columns with capitals once

supported the roof, which jutted out into the central courtyard with its large gushing fountain; two other fountains were situated in front of the pillars facing the Triclinium. The Xystus is closed by an apsidal nymphaeum with three niches that once contained fountains continually fed with water from above. In the area to the right, behind the apse, there was the kitchen (30/a) serving the Triclinium. Moreover, a corridor (30/b) connected the four-sided portico to the Xystus.

The mosaics are typical of the Imperial period and portray animals (lions, tigers, horses, wolves, etc.) surrounded by acanthus leaves. You can still just about see the frescoes that once covered the whole inside of the colonnade with life size figures.

From the Triclinium you could see the famous hetaerae twirling in the courtyard surrounded by fountains, water spouts, light and music. These pretty girls were

not only excellent dancers but were also experts in the art of love.

There are six rooms opening onto the sides of the portico, three on either side.

These rooms were probably used by guests to retire with the hetaerae after the lavish banquets.

The mosaics in the rooms to the right of the Triclinium depict the transportation and pressing of grapes by cupids. In the vestibule (31) which leads into the other two rooms you will see, on the right (32), cupids harvesting grapes and, in the centre of the room, a medallion portraying the god Dionysus;

on the left (33), the mosaic, no longer visible, depicted the growing of vines. On the other side of the Ovoid Portico there are three rooms with the same layout as those just described: one room acted as a vestibule (34), with pieces of mosaic depicting fishing cupids, and this led on the right (35) and on the left (36) into two bedrooms, in which only traces of the mosaics remain.

On this page: the mosaics in the Xystus depicting lions, flowers, horses, bears, etc.

TRICLINIUM (37)

The Triclinium is a large square dining room with three apses and an entrance with two columns. This is where the dominus received his important guests. In the apse there are lecti tricliniares, sofas made of stone, or more often bronze, with cushions, but without any kind of headboard or backrest. The guests rested on their elbows while tasting the drinks set out on the table (cartibulum), which was originally in stone but was later replaced by slabs of marble. The origin of the name triclinium derives from the ancient habit of setting out three sofas perpendicular to one another, with a table in the centre.

The mosaics in the central part of the room depict the twelve mythological labours of Hercules and have such a good sense of continuity and rhythm that they lend the whole work an air of realism and drama: you will notice the skittish horses of Diomedes unseating their riders who have been struck by Hercules; the dragon with iridescent scales defending the apples of the Hesperides; the Cretan bull, first captured and then released by Hercules; the slain Nemean lion; the Lernaean Hydra, depicted with a single female head; Geryon, the monster with three bodies; the Erymanthian boar in the large vase; the Arcadian stag; the

Bottom: two-columned entrance to Triclinium.

pitchfork and the water used to clean the Augean stables; Cerberus with three heads. In the centre of this beautiful mosaic you can Diomedes being unseated from his black horse.

The only labours not depicted are the slaying of the Stymphalian birds and the capture of the girdle of Hippolyta, Queen of the Amazons.

The mosaics in the apse to the left depict the glorification of Hercules, who is shown naked with a beard and a leopard skin, while Zeus places a laurel wreath on his head

It is thought that this mosaic represents the victories gained by the Emperor Maximianus (Herculius) in Germany (kneeling at his feet, on the right, is the genius of the Rhine), in Britannia (the rebel Carausius at Hercules' feet) and in Africa (the apples of the Hesperides, on the left, which are thought to have been found in Morocco).

In the entrance opposite you can see, on the left, the metamorphosis of the nymph Daphne into a laurel tree and, on the right, the metamorphosis of Cyparissus into a cypress tree. In the central apse you will see five giants who had challenged Zeus struck by arrows fired by Hercules.

The arrows were poisonous because they had been

Top: in the central apse five giants who challenged Zeus are struck by Hercules' poison arrows.

63

On this page: the giants' agony.

dipped in the blood of the centaur Nessus. There is a marble covered pedestal on which a marble torso of Hercules stands.

Under the giants are Hesione, who is pointing at a sea

monster mortally wounded by Hercules' arrows, and Endymion lying down and pointing at the moon. Endymion was condemned by Zeus to sleep for thirty years because he had courted Hera.

The apse to the right has a mosaic depicting the triumph of the Dionysian powers over Lycurgus, King of Thrace. You can also see the metamorphosis of Bacchant Ambrosia, turned into a vine by Dionysus.

The branches of the vine cling to the King's legs as he tries to kill Ambrosia with a double-headed axe.

Having finished your visit to the Triclinium, you head back the way you came. Once outside, you will see the secondary aqueduct (38), the tank for water collection (39) and a small octagonal latrine (40), which was used exclusively by members of the owner's family. This latrine is extremely well preserved and only the seats situated above the sewer are missing. The walls were frescoed and the mosaic depicts a vase containing branches with ivy leaves.

To the right of the entrance there is a water tank that provided water to flush the sewer. Climbing the small iron staircase you now enter the rooms used by the domina.

DIAETA OF ARION (41)

This is the large sitting-room used by the mistress of the Villa. She spent her afternoons here, listening to music or chatting to other members of the family. It is a rectangular room with two columns at the entrance and an apse with windows.

The mosaic on the floor portrays the myth of Arion, who succeeds in enchanting some dolphins with his lyre and enticing them around the ship on which he was held prisoner and was about to be killed.

To escape, he threw himself into the sea and was carried to safety by one of the dolphins. In the mosaic Arion, a famous poet and musician from the island of Lesbos, is surrounded by mythological marine animals, winged cupids, fish, Nereides, hippocampi, tritons, tigers, panthers, deer, wolves, lions and by centaurs carrying caskets of pearls.

The prophet-poet Arion, is playing his lyre while seated on a dolphin's back and with a large cloak draped across his shoulder. The mosaic in the lunette of the apse depicts the head of the god Oceanus, with a beard and long flowing hair, decorated with two crab claws.

Prawns, polyps and other sea creatures can be seen coming out of his mouth. To reach this room from the Large Hunting Ambulacrum it was necessary to pass through a colonnaded atrium, which served as access to the rooms used by the children of the dominus and to the sitting-room.

SEMICIRCULAR COLONNADED ATRIUM (41/A)

This was reached from the Large Hunting Ambulacrum through two entrances placed on either side of an elegant nymphaeum. In the Graeco-Roman world places with plentiful water were consecrated to the nymphs and had a religious significance. It was only late on in the imperial age that nymphaea became common in wealthy Roman households. These rooms were often decorated with columns, fountains, frescoes and statues. Jets of cool water and ingenious fountains provided a place to sit and relax during the hottest part of the day. Four semicircular columns with Ionic capitals supported the compluvium, which collected rainwater and channelled it into the impluvium. This was an opening in the ceiling of the atrium through which light entered, as well as rainwater,

which was collected in the tank on the floor. The atrium served as access to the bedrooms used by the children of the dominus and for the Diaeta of Arion. The mosaics depict winged cupids in boats fishing with nets, fish traps and harpoons or swimming in the sea and playing with ducklings. In the upper part of the mosaic you will notice buildings linked by long colonnades.

VESTIBULE OF THE SMALL CIRCUS (42)

From the walkway along which you pass, you will be able to see, on the left, the Vestibule called "of the Small Circus". This room is jokingly decorated with mosaics depicting the caricature of a circus. The chariots are driven by children and drawn by white geese, red flamingos, blue wading birds and green doves. The feathers are coloured to represent the four factions or teams: albata, russata, veneta and prasina. The winner was awarded the victory palm leaf.

CUBICLE OF MUSICIANS AND ACTORS (43)

Connecting with the Vestibule (42) is a rectangular room which was probably used as a bedroom by the owner's daughter. The apse is decorated by two columns, of which only the bases remain today. The mosaic in the apse is inspired by a pagan festival that was held in spring in honour of the goddess Flora (protector of women giving birth and goddess of flowers). During this festival games and performances were held in order to favour the fertility of the land. Two girls are portrayed either side of a tree, engaged in making rose wreaths. Above the tree there is an ivy leaf, symbol of the herculea dynasty of the Emperor Maximianus. Either side of the bases of the columns the mosaic depicts two baskets containing rose wreaths, four palm leaves and two small bags. These were prizes for the winners of the competitions for musicians and actors. In the rest of the room the mosaics show three scenes. The upper scene portrays a quartet playing a lyre, a small portable organ, a double flute and a reed-pipe. The scene is completed by a character, maybe a judge, wearing a white trimmed tunic and raising his arm to signal the start of the competition. In the central scene, apart from actors, musicians with large drums and singers, there is a red disc surmounted by five small circles with Greek letters indicating musical notes. In the lower scene you will see a group of boys and girls dressed in long tunics. Here, there is another disc with more notes.

VESTIBULE OF EROS AND PAN (44)

You continue your visit with the two rooms on the other side of the atrium, symmetrical to those described above (42/43). These are rooms used by one of the children of the dominus. The first room is a rectangular vestibule reached by passing through a doorway in the semicircular atrium. The walls show traces of pictorial decoration. In this room the mosaics depict the strug-

Top: the Vestibule of the Small Circus decorated with mosaics depicting a caricature of a circus.

gle between Pan and Eros. Among the onlookers you will notice, on the left, as well as the referee of the match in his red cloak, a satyr and three maenads; behind Eros, on the right, a woman with a young man, a girl and two servants who, for various reasons, some researchers believe are members of the imperial family. In the centre you can see a table with vases and date palm branches and, at the bottom, bags full of money, the value of which is indicated in writing. According to tradition Pan, a venerated Greek god, was born from the union between Hermes and Dryope. The divine child was born with a bearded face, horns and cloven hoofs and was abandoned by his frightened mother. Hermes wrapped him in a hare skin and took him onto Mount Olympus. All the gods were happy to accept him and he was given the name of Pan (everything). Pan brought with him the lively joy of primeval pastoral feasts. Mythical tradition talks of Pan's numerous love affairs. Among others, one with Selene, the moon, who first rejected him and was then seduced by him; with the nymphs Pitis, Syrinx and Echo, who changed, respectively, into a pine-tree, a reed-bed and a voice, in order to escape from him. In particular, in the case of Syrinx, who changed into a reed-bed, the god Pan cut seven reeds of different lengths in remembrance of his beloved and used them to make his pastoral flute, which he called Syrinx.

BEDROOM OF THE HUNTING CHILDREN (45)

From the Vestibule it was possible to enter the bedroom occupied by the son of the dominus. This room has a rectangular alcove (the internal part of the room), which was once decorated with two columns. The mosaic in the alcove has a floral theme and shows three scenes. In the upper part two girls are collecting roses in baskets. In the second scene a girl is carrying baskets full of flowers, while another girl, seated on a basket, is plaiting roses with ribbons hanging down from the tree. In the lower scene a boy is carrying a pole across his shoulders with baskets full of flowers hanging from the ends. In the anteroom the mosaic shows three humoristic hunting scenes involving children. In the first and third of these scenes children are seen hunting hares, ducks, peacocks and bustards, while in the central one it is the

animals, including household pets, that are chasing after the children. In order to continue your visit you go outside and walk to the left along the side of the Basilica (46), which can be observed from the exterior.

BASILICA (46)

The imposing Basilica is the largest room in the Villa and was reached by passing through the Large Hunting Ambulacrum. A few steps and two massive pink granite columns marked the entrance to a Basilica worthy of an Emperor. This is the room used in the Greek and Roman worlds for official receptions and meetings. The basilica was the place where the basileus (emperor or king) reigned, imparted justice and received important guests. The Byzantines later turned it into a church and the winged cupids became angels and cherubs. The walls were once decorated with beautiful marble, remains of which can be seen at the base of the walls. The floor was originally paved in beautiful white marble with inlay work (opus sectile), but today only a tiny part of this original floor can be seen. The coloured inlays formed geometrical patterns similar to those in the curia where the Senate met in Rome. In the centre of the room there are the remains of a porphyry rota. In the apse, slightly higher than the rest of the room, was the Emperor's throne, but today you can only see the brick stall in which it was positioned. In front of the stall there is part of another porphyry rota, decorated with small coloured palms and acanthus flowers. Some experts believe that the presence of the rotae is further evidence of the fact that the Villa belonged to Maximianus, since rotae were to be found only in buildings used by the Emperor. To the sides of the apse there were two columns, of which only the bases remain.

Behind the throne there is a large niche which housed a gigantic statue of Hercules. Only the head of the statue has survived and is now to be found in the Museum. Continuing on your way around the perimeter of the Basilica, after passing through a doorway leading outside, a metal staircase takes you into the apartments used by the dominus.

Vestibule of Polyphemus (47)

This luxurious room was entered through the Large Hunting Ambulacrum. The room was used as a vestibule for the bedrooms (48-49) occupied by the dominus and by the domina of the Villa. The walls are decorated with moulded squares and the entrance doorway still has the four holes for the door hinges. The real beauty of this room, however, is in the mosaic, which portrays the Cyclops Polyphemus and Ulysses with some of his companions in a cave. The enormous Cyclops, with three eyes, a beard and long hair, is seated on a rock, naked and with a ram on one of his legs, while Ulysses hands him a crater full of wine. This Homeric theme is often to be found in Roman mosaics.

The Cyclopes

Experts on ancient myths and legend distinguish between four types of Cyclopes. The Uranian Cyclopes, sons of Uranus and Gaia (Heaven and Earth), belong to the first divine generation, that of the Giants. They have a single eye in the centre of their foreheads and are characterised by their strength and dexterity.

In Alexandrian poetry the Cyclopes are considered to be blacksmiths and artisans who made weapons for the gods. They live in the Aeolian Islands, Sicily or the Phlegraean Fields, near Naples. In Sicily they have an underground forge where they work noisily. It is their panting

and the noise of their hammers and anvils that can be heard in the depths of Sicily's volcanoes. The fire from their forge lights up the sky on the top of Etna.

Next, we have the builder Cyclopes. These Cyclopes (said to be from Lycia) are reputed to be responsible for the construction of some of the prehistoric monuments in Greece (the fortifications of Tiryns) and in Sicily (the Cyclopean walls of Cefalù and of Erice), made of huge blocks which seem to be impossible for humans to manage, given their weight and dimensions.

The first Greek settlers in Sicily thought they had identified the skeletons of these Giants in some caves near Siracusa. Presumably it was the skull of a species of dwarf elephant that once lived in Sicily and had a hole in its forehead, leading the Greeks to believe it was a Cyclops.

Finally, the Sicilian Cyclopes are those mentioned in the Odyssey. The most famous Cyclops is definitely Polyphemus, son of Poseidon and of the nymph Toosa.

Ulisses and Polyphemus

This Homeric epic was written down about seven centuries before the birth of Christ, but cannot be traced to a single identifiable author. Between 1200 and 800BC poets composed epics and passed them on orally and these were later collected together on the orders of Pisistratus, the tyrant of Athens. The Odyssey tells of the vicissitudes of Ulysses during his return voyage to Ithaca, the island of his birth, after having taken part in the siege and sacking of Troy. It was Ulysses' brilliant idea to build the famous "Trojan Horse". Blown off course by a storm, Ulysses and his companions land on the island of the Cyclopes.

The exact geographical location of the meeting between Ulysses and Polyphemus is not certain; the popular contenders are Acitrezza, at the foot of Mount Etna, and Drakotes, on the island of Crete. In the past, some researchers claimed to have identified the place as Erice.

The meeting between Ulysses and Polyphemus represents the universal metaphor of the struggle between good and evil, between brains and brawn.

Ulysses tells Alcinous, King of the Phaeacians, how he discovered Polyphemus' cave, while exploring the island with his companions. Ulysses waited for the Cyclops to return but Polyphemus herded his flock of sheep into the cave and then closed off the entrance with a huge rock, after having devoured two of Ullysses' companions. The giant promised that Ulysses would be the last one to be eaten, as a sign of gratitude for the gift of wine received. With the wine, Ulysses managed to make the giant drunk and get him to fall asleep. During the night Ulysses and his companions used a red hot poker to blind Polyphemus in his only eye. Blinded and crazed with pain, Polyphemus called for

help from the other Cyclopes. They raced outside the cave and asked who was trying to kill him, to which he replied "Nobody". This is what Ulysses had told Polyphemus he was called while the giant was drinking the wine.

The other Cyclopes, unaware of this clever trick played by Ulysses, went away feeling angry because they had been woken up for nothing.

In the morning, when Polyphemus opened the cave to let out his flock, the Greeks tied themselves under the bellies of the sheep and succeeded in escaping, even though Polyphemus felt the back of each sheep.

Once they were free and their ship had set sail, Ulysses shouted his real name to Polyphemus.

The Cyclops was furious and tore huge rocks out of the hillside and threw them in the direction from which the voice came. After surviving this adventure Ulysses resumed his homeward voyage to Ithaca.

BEDROOM OF FRUIT (48)

A few metres further on and you come to the quadrangular room used by the mistress of the house as a

bedroom and which was entered from the Vestibule (47).

The alcove is apsidal, with two painted stone pillars, of which only the bases remain.

The walls were once frescoed: you can just about make out the figure of a cupid on the southern wall.

The mosaics decorating the floor are magnificent: three superimposed squares form a twelve-pointed star, encompassing nine laurel wreaths with different kinds of fruit (pears, lemons, peaches, grapes, pomegranates, prickly pears). In the alcove the mosaic depicts lunettes in which you can see thin delicate flowers.

Facing page: detail of the erotic scene.

BEDROOM WITH EROTIC SCENE (49)

Moving to the left, you come into the bedroom used by the dominus.

This room has a rectangular alcove with two stone pil-

lars. The frescoes decorating the walls show satyrs and maenads.

These are mythological characters who were part of the entourage of Dionysus (Bacchus for the Romans), god of wine and love, who often enjoyed indulging himself in orgies. The floor of the alcove has a mosaic with a geometrical pattern of circles which overlap and form four-petalled flowers.

Between the pillars there is a scene showing children, apparently playing with balls. The mosaic in the rest of the room has a woven pattern of geometrical shapes and fig-

ures. In the centre of this you will see a laurel wreath with the famous erotic scene: a scantily-clad woman embracing a young man and kissing him. Squares with colourful plaits and hexagons containing personifications of the four seasons form four eight-pointed stars to either side of the room.

Within these are laurel wreaths containing masks representing the Saturnalia, feasts in honour of the god Saturn.

Piazza Armerina

The history of the town of Piazza (Armerina was added in 1862) began in Norman times, but the area was already inhabited in prehistoric times, as is demonstrated by the archaeological finds on Monte Navone and, above all, on Montagna di Marzo. The area must have flourished in the Roman era: this can be seen from the splendid Roman Villa Casale, dating from the early 4th century AD, with its world famous mosaic floors.

The Normans came to Sicily in 1061 and started a long war against the Arabs, which ended in 1130 with their conquest of the Island and the

beginning of the reign of Roger II. In the first half of the 12th century, Piazza was probably situated in the Casale area and its inhabitants, who had never mixed well with the Saracen populations in the surrounding area, naturally viewed the Normans' pro-Saracen policy with mistrust. Thus, the population took part in the revolt of 1160 by the feudal lords, led by Roger Sclavo, the illegitimate son of Count Simon Aleramico, and by Tancredi d'Altavilla, the illegitimate son of Roger, Duke of Puglia and brother of King William I, massacring the Saracens who lived in the area. In 1161 the town was conquered by King William I (the

Bad), son of Roger, who he had succeeded, and he took revenge by razing the town to the ground. The survivors scattered to the outlying villages that had escaped William's wrath and lived there until they gained permission to rebuild a new town on the Mira hill, the present day district of Monte.

There is little information to be found about Piazza in the rest of the 12th century but it seems certain that after the end of the Norman domination, in 1194, the town became rich, prosperous and important again under Emperor Frederick of Swabia

During the Swabian domination the town was home to the Knights Templar Hospitallers and of the Holy Sepulchre, participated in the Crusade of 1227, was chosen as seat of the National Court of the Kingdom in Sicily and took part in the General Parliament of Foggia.

With the arrival of the Angevins, a period of oppression and suffering began in Sicily, during which the town took part in the Vespers War against the French government of Charles of Anjou.

In 1296 Piazza hosted the meeting of the Sicilian Parliament at which Frederick II of Aragon was proclaimed King of Sicily. The new king approved the "customs" of the town, which are still preserved today in the "Book of privileges", in the Municipal Library.

After the death of Frederick II Sicily experienced a period of disputes and fighting between various factions of noblemen but Piazza, despite participating in these disputes, maintained a prestigious role, especially from an economic point of view. In 1348 the population of the town was decimated by the plague and this was when, according to tradition, the standard of Our Lady of Victories, later to become patron of the town, was found. The Aragonese Castle used by King Frederick II, Maria and Martin of Aragon was probably built around this time too. The Spanish domination lasted three more centuries.

FROM THE SPANISH DOMINATION TO THE PRESENT DAY

The reign of Alphonse of Aragon brought a period of peace to Sicily but it was also a period of reduced autonomy, because Sicily became an outlying province of the huge Spanish Empire. Piazza first became a feud of Peter of Aragon but, later, it regained its privileges. Over this period of time the town grew in size considerably and was made the seat of a "comarca" that included the feuds of Mazzarino, Pietraperzia, Terranova, Bufera, Barrafranca and Aidone. The cultural and economic life of the town was particularly active, so much so that it was described by Emperor Charles V as an "extremely wealthy town". The 17th and 18th centuries saw the town reach the height of its splendour, thanks to the construction of numerous Baroque buildings, churches, monasteries and a hospital. Unfortunately, a slow decline set in when the nobility began to move from Piazza to Palermo and Naples, even though it was chosen as seat of a new diocese in 1817 and was made seat of an administrative district within the new province of Caltanissetta. During the revolutionary uprising of 1848 the local nobility joined the Committee of public safety, but it took ten years for the Italian tricolour to be raised on the town hall. During the First World War many men from Piazza made an important contribution and General A. Cascino was awarded the Gold Medal for military valour.

Apart from a few rare occasions the 20th century saw little done to try to revitalise the town and allow it to regain the important role it had historically enjoyed. The decision to make Enna the new provincial capital put an end to any aspirations the town may have had to become a significant political centre.

Carmen Scalisi

Bottom: the monument dedicated to General A. Cascino.

SIATE LA VALANGA CHE
CASCINO

DISCOVERING THE TOWN

You experience a feeling of wonder when you catch sight of the cupola of the Cathedral rising up above the roof-tops, as you make your way along

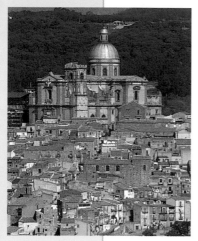

via Roma and into Piazza Garibaldi. It towers above the façade of the Palazzo di città (18th century), the Palazzo Capodarso (18th century), the church of Fundrò (17th century) and the ex-Benedictine monastery (17th century), almost as if to underline its architectural superiority over all the other monuments of the town. All these buildings are notable for their simplicity and elegance and, although they can each be admired independently, they can also be considered as a single architectural complex. Each building fits harmoniously into the framework of the beautiful Piazza Garibaldi, the pulsating heart of the town. From this square streets lead off into the old town, where every stone has a story to tell if you look carefully and appreciate the intrinsic beauty of the buildings.

Top: the majestic cupola of the Cathedral.

The Palazzo di città is a simple 18th century building with an elegant baroque façade, characterised by a gallery that runs its entire length and by wide symmetrical windows. The whole effect blends in well with the yellow tuff portal of the adjacent church of Fundrò. High up in the façade a modern clock is surmounted by two bells, which mark the passage of time with their chimes in the 17th-18th century atmosphere of Piaz-

za Garibaldi. This building was the seat of a Senate, a privilege granted to the town by King Ferdinand of Bourbon in 1777, when it was made administrative centre for a group of six towns. Nowadays the building houses a private club, called the Cultural Circle, on the ground floor and on the first floor there is a chamber used for meet-

ings of the Town Council. The ceiling of this chamber is decorated with frescoes by Gioacchino Martorana from Palermo.

Palazzo Capodarso is an impressive example of 18th century architecture, with a solid Baroque façade decorated with elegant stone sculptures. It is believed that the design of the building provided for another floor to be constructed, but this was never done.

The Baroque Church of Fundrò (Saint Rocco), dating back to 1613, stands at the top of peculiar round-shaped staircase and is characterised by a sturdy portal in tuff, richly decorated with inlays. The church was initially dedicated to Saint Rocco but in 1622 it was entrusted to the Benedictine monks from the abbey of Fundrò, a country district about ten kilometres outside the town, when their monastery was destroyed by fire and they were forced to seek alternative accommodation.

The single nave of the interior of the church does not

Top: the Palazzo di Città.

Bottom: Panoramic view of the town.

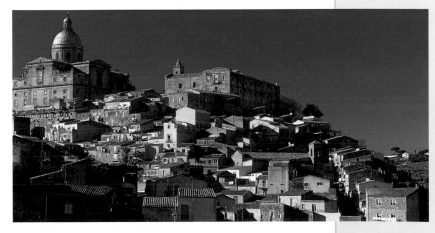

give the visitor the same impression of grandeur created by the portal.

Inside the church you can see several 17th century canvases and an interesting marble statue of Our Lady, positioned above the main altar, which probably comes from the old country abbey.

Curiously, there is a sundial above the portal, seemingly in competition with the modern clock on the adjacent Palazzo di città.

Next to the church is the ex-Benedictine Monastery, now the Town Hall, which you enter by passing through a sculpted arch, leading into a pretty courtyard that has been skilfully restored. In Piazza Fundrò stands Palazzo Demani di Canicarao, now home to the tourist information centre.

*Facing page:
Church of
Fundrò.*

*Bottom: the
Castellina Tower.*

Behind the ex-Benedictine monastery is the Castellina district, one of the four historical districts of the town, so called because it was situated at the foot of a mediaeval castle that stood on the site of the present day monastery of Saint Francis. At the centre of the district stands the Church of Saint Veneranda, which was founded in 1180, although the present day façade dates from 1650.

The lowest part of the district is closed off by the old Castellina Tower (1337) and by a stretch of fortified walls with a wide opening, serving as a gateway into the district.

PIAZZA DUOMO

Returning up via Cavour, you come to Piazza S. Rosalia, which has recently been restored.

Here you will see Palazzo Trigona di Canicarao (17th century) on the right, a noble 17th century residence with a crenellated façade and a wide portal surmounted by a large balcony bearing an eagle with a shield, the emblem of the Trigona di Canicarao family.

The side of the building overlooking largo Demani is more attractive but the interior, unfortunately, bears little resemblance to the original.

The splendour that must once have distinguished it has been lost, due to numerous alterations of a questionable nature carried out by the various owners over the years, leaving little trace of its past glory.

The self-supporting stone stairway overlooking the courtyard is particularly attractive.

Palazzo Trigona.

A little further on, in Piazza Calarco, you will find the majestic ex-Monastery of Saint Francis (17th century). This impressive piece of architecture was built in the early 1600s and the façade overlooking via Cavour is characterised by a Baroque style balcony attributed to the Gagini brothers.

From 1870 to 1999 it housed the town's hospital.

Inside there is a square cloister, probably predating the building.

The conical top of the bell tower is in colourful majolica.

Further on, you arrive in Piazza Duomo, dominated by the imposing mass of the Cathedral.

It took nearly three centuries to build this colossal monument, with its majestic portal and tortile columns.

It was constructed thanks to Baron Marco Trigona, who made a bequest on his death in 1598 to pay for a more impressive religious building than the previous 15th century Cathedral.

The Gothic-Catalan style bell tower of this previous building remains, although the upper part underwent alterations in the 16th century.

Bell tower in Gothic-Catalan style

The interior has a Latin cross layout, a single wide nave with lateral communicating chapels.

It houses numerous works of art, including a 17th century canvas of the assumption of the Virgin by F. Paladini, situated above the altar in the left-hand transept, the Martyrdom of Saint Agatha by Jacopo Ligozzi and a wooden Cross by an unknown artist of the Antonello school, conventionally called Master of the Cross of Piazza Armerina.

The Cross is painted on both sides (Christ crucified on the front and Christ resurrected on the back).

In the centre of the same square there is a statue of Baron Marco Trigona, portrayed offering the Cathedral to the town.

Facing page: Our Lady of Victories.

Overlooking the square is Palazzo Trigona della Floresta (18th century), which it is hoped will soon house the town's archaeological museum.
The main façade is characterised by a refined portal,

a series of wide windows on the first floor and long balconies on the top floor.
High up, the eagle of the Trigona family stands out.

Top: an attractive caryatid.

Bottom: characteristic street in the Monte district.

MONTE

Passing along via Monte, the old "strata mastra" (main street), you will see numerous buildings worthy of note: Palazzo Geraci, the Monastery of the Trinity, the building traditionally believed to have been the residence of Baron M. Trigona, with its refined Gothic-Catalan portal and the Palazzo belonging to the Marquises of Roccabianca, unfortunately badly restored.

The Monte district is a classical example of Norman town planning, with side streets leading of the main street in a fish-bone pattern. At the end of via Monte you can visit the 17th century Church of the Guardian Angels, with its rich frescoes, and the Church of Our Lady of the Chain (12th century), previously known as Saint Nicholas al Monte. The external architecture of the church is very plain; inside, the chapel of Our Lady of the Chain is worth visiting. Along via Crocifisso you enter the district of the same name. Here you will find the Church of the Crucifix, which houses several canvases of particular interest.

There is also an 18th century wooden choir with a 17th canvas portraying Saint Dominica on the left-hand wall, an 18th century pipe organ and an ancient Crucifix that has been used in processions for centuries.

The nearby Church of St. Martin of Tours was the first church founded by the Normans in the new town of Platia in 1163 and is dedicated to their patron Saint. It stands in the lowest part of the Monte district and was the Cathedral of the town until the 15th century. Very little remains of the original building, only the side

100

portals with ogival arches. The present day façade dates back to 1598.

The interior has a single nave with a beautiful 19th century wooden ceiling and a 15th century marble baptismal font.

PIAZZA CASTELLO

This pretty square is situated in the southern area of the old Monte district.

Apart from the Aragonese castle from which it takes its name, there are also some elegant noble residences (Velardita and Roccazzella from the 18th century and Starrabba from the 19th century) and the delightful church of Our Lady of the Snow (17th century).

The Aragonese Castle was built at the end of the 14th century and was the residence of King Martin I of Aragon for a long time. It has a quadrilateral layout with quadrangular towers and

The Aragonese Castle.

Top: Palazzo Starabba.

Bottom: Church of Our Lady of the Snow.

looks over a wide valley. Only two of the three original floors are still in existence.

The small Church of Our Lady of the Snow is situated on the western side of the square, adjacent to the Augustan monastery (17th century).

The lovely white stucco decorations make the interior particularly attractive and it also houses numerous interesting paintings.

VIA VITTORIO EMANUELE

Via Vittorio Emanuele connects Piazza Castello with Piazza Garibaldi and along this street you will find the ex-Jesuit College, with the adjacent church of Saint Ignatius (17th century), and the elegantly shaped church of Saint Anne (18th century).

The Jesuit College dates back to the early 1600s, when the Jesuits came to the town.

Inside you can see a characteristic arcade with high brick pillars.

Nowadays the building houses the Municipal Library.

The square overlooked by the College and the surrounding monuments can be considered a jewel in the field of town planning and a perfect example of architectural harmony.

The 17th century Church of Saint Ignatius, adjacent to the Jesuit College, is higher up than the street level and you enter it by climbing steps in carved stone. The façade is made of pressed brick and has a convex shape, similar to that of the nearby church of Saint Anne, with an attractive entrance portal.

The interior has recently been restored, saving it from the gradual decline into which it had fallen and restoring its dignity.

The Church of Saint Anne has a characteristic octagonal shape and was built in the early 1700s. it is entered by climbing a double stone staircase.

The interior has, unfortunately, been completely destroyed and nothing remains of its original splendour.

However, it would regain some of its dignity with restoration, albeit late, if only to make it fit in with the attractive exterior and with the other beautiful monuments in the district.

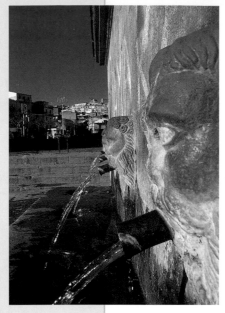

THE CANALI DISTRICT

You now arrive in Piazza Garibaldi, from where you can easily visit the neighbouring district of Canali, an old part of the town, inhabited until 1492 by Jews (Giudecca) and once the commercial and productive heart of the town. The district is located in the lowest lying part of the town, where the abundant fresh water supply was provided by the "Fonte dei Canali", which fed the mediaeval washhouse. Near the Fonte (fountain) there is a small church dedicated to Saint Lucy, probably built in 1685 on the site of a pre-existing 14th century synagogue. In the higher part of the district you can visit the 17th century Church of Itria, with an elegant Baroque portal in sandstone, which was the second parish church to be built in the town after Saint Martin's.

Top and Bottom: the ancient Canali Fountain.

VIA UMBERTO

After turning into via Umberto I, you immediately find the 17th century Church of the Holy Souls in Purgatory. If you follow the side street alongside it you come to the square of Sant'Antonio, which takes its name from the church, now deconsecrated, dedicated to

the patron Saint of pets. Standing on this square you will see the Church of St. Vincent and the ex-Monastery of Saint Dominic (17th century); both of these buildings are part of the larger complex of the Bishop's Palace. The ex-Dominican Monastery is now home to the episcopal Seminary and has a beautiful cloister with stone columns. In front of the entrance to the Seminary you turn from via Cammarata into via Umberto I, where you will find the beautiful Palazzo Mandrascati, which has unfortunately been poorly altered and restored. You will also see the ex-Convent of St. Chiara, completely gutted in a haphazard attempt at restoration, as well as other interesting noble residences.

Top: Tower of the Holy Father in the Piano Teatini.

PIANO TEATINI

Largo San Giovanni is overlooked by the façade of the 14th century Church of Saint John, with its lovely 18th century frescoes by the Flemish artist G. Borremans.

Adjacent to this stands the Church of Saint Lawrence al Patrisanto, commonly called the Church of the Theatines. You can still see some remains of the primitive

Bottom: Church of St. Stephen.

mediaeval structure in the side portal and in the ogival windows, similar to those in the beautiful church of St. Andrew.

In the three naves of the interior you can admire marvellous frescoes and Baroque stuccoes. The numerous canvases that once decorated the lateral altars are now kept elsewhere.

On this page: the façade and boxes of the Garibaldi Theatre.

In Piazza Martiri d'Ungheria (formerly piano Padre Santo) you will see the Tower of the Holy Father, part of the mediaeval town walls. The Tower shows evident signs of the alterations made in various eras, from the late Gothic portal with archivolt and Baroque balcony on the first floor to the Renaissance window on the second floor.

Nearby you can visit the 17th century Church of Saint Stephen and the Commendam of the Knights of Malta, built in the 12th century and now used for cultural events. The Church of Saint Stephen, built in the

late 16th and early 17th century, is characterised by a simple brickwork façade, broken only by an elegant portal in carved tuff, preceded by a trapezoidal stairway, and by a richly decorated bell tower in finely sculpted tuff.

Nearby you will find the Garibaldi Theatre, which dates from the early 1900s and has an elegant façade, which fits in harmoniously with the other monuments in the area. It is rightly considered a 'little jewel', small though it may be, thanks to its attractive design and refined frescoes.

Soon after passing the monument dedicated to General A. Cascino, a First World War hero, you come to the 16th century Church of St. Peter, with a beautiful 18th century wooden coffered ceiling.

Top: Church of St. Peter.

Bottom: detail of the Church of St. Peter.

107

Church of the Carmine and Cloister.

THE CASALOTTO DISTRICT

The rural district of Casalotto once belonged to the Branciforti family of Mazzarino and only became part of the town of Piazza in 1598. There used to be an oratory here, dedicated to Saint Phillip Neri, which became a sacramental church in the 17th century.

The Church of Saint Phillip Neri is located in the square of the same name and has a plain façade with an inlaid sandstone portal. In the lower part of the district stands the 17th century Church of the Carmine, with the adjacent convent, which was built on the ruins of the 15th century church of St. Albert. The Gothic-Catalan style bell tower of this latter church still stands today. The 16th century cloister is interesting, as is the marble statue of Our Lady by A. Gagini situated above the portal of the church.

PIAZZA ARMERINA AND SURROUNDING AREA

Outside the town there are several buildings of architectural interest worth visiting.
The Grand Priory of Saint Andrew, founded in the

early 1100s, is a beautiful example of mediaeval Sicilian art.
The interior was restored in the last century and this restoration has brought to light a series of attractive frescoes dating from the 12th to the 15th century.

Frescoes in the Grand Priorate of Saint Andrew.

The Church of Our Lady of Mercy (16th century) and the adjacent ex-Capuchin Monastery (17th century) are situated in a panoramic position on piano S. Ippolito. This complex is built in a very simple and essential style.

The church has a single nave and houses a valuable 16th century painting on wood portraying Our Lady of Mercy by Antonio da Padova, numerous canvases depicting Saints and a notable carved wooden altar, surmounted by a large painting of Our Lady and two male figures holding a tray with the town of Piazza on it.

Top: painting in the Capuchin Monastery.

Bottom: wooden altar..

The Convent of Santa Maria di Gesù was founded in the early 1400s, but the present poorly maintained building probably dates from the following century.

The porch with pillars serves as a base for a gallery with segmental arches supported by thin

columns. The Sanctuary of Piazza Vecchia is so called because, according to tradition, this is where the old Piazza (Plutia) was situated, before being destroyed by William I.

This is where the image of Our Lady of Victories was found in 1348.

This image is now kept in the Cathedral.

The Sanctuary houses, however, a copy of the sacred icon, which is carried in procession from Piazza Vecchia to the Church of the Guardian Angels on the last Sunday in April every year. It is then carried back on 3rd May, a feast day which is celebrated by the whole population.

Finally, the woods around the town are very popular with the locals and are used for leisure activities, such as jogging or picking mushrooms and wild asparagus.

Facing page: the woods surrounding the town.

At a place called Ronza there is a park of the same name, which attracts visitors from all around the area for picnics and day trips.

Bottom: Pietra Tower.

In the Bellia woods an important livestock market is held on the 28th of each month, where farm equipment is also sold.

Vincenzo Giusto

Festivals and Traditions

Festivals in Piazza Armerina are influenced, as in the rest of Sicily, by the various periods of domination experienced over the centuries, especially the Spanish domination. Genuine piety and deep-seated faith, along with a touch of superstition, create the mixture characterising the solemn religious celebrations, particularly the traditional processions. Unlike other places in Sicily, however, the religious festivals in Piazza Armerina are characterised by a common sense of dignity. The most important festivals are considered the high points of the year. People here often plan their activities, work, holidays and so on in consideration of the festival dates: "I'll see to it after the festival!" is a frequently heard expression, giving you an idea of how eagerly awaited the festivals are, be they sacred or profane occasions.

During the Baroque Carnival there are costume parades inspired by that period of history: ladies, knights and other characters perform a kind of grotesque pantomime that attracts large crowds. In the evening Baroque dances and competitions between representatives of the four districts of the town are held in the beautiful setting of Piazza Duomo.

The celebrations for Holy Week in Piazza Armerina, as all over the Island, play a particularly important role in the expression of popular religious feeling. This is particularly so during the celebration of the Easter rites. In the various churches of the town it is customary to prepare the "sepolcri" (specially decorated chapels), which are visited by large numbers of people until very late on the Thursday evening. On Good Friday the celebrations take on a dramatic air. People congregate in the Church of the Most Holy Crucifix, in the Monte district, to witness

the laying of the dead Christ onto the litter on which he will be carried in procession. The litter is carried by young men dressed in white and is followed by the Virgin in a black cape, carried on the shoulders of girls dressed in black. A unique characteristic of the Good Friday procession in Piazza Armerina is the presence of a Christ on the cross with a globe at his feet, symbolising divine protection for the world. Drama and a sense of sorrow are added to the proceedings by the "lamenti", mediaeval dirges sung along the route.

The festival of Piazza Vecchia, celebrated on 3rd May, is original and especially interesting. In the morning the Standard of Our Lady leaves the Church of Angels in Monte to the pealing of bells and a warm welcome from the crowds outside, accompanied by the horsemen of the victorious district in the previous year's Palio. The people then follow the standard on foot as far as the Sanctuary adjacent to the

ruins of the so-called castle of Count Roger, about five kilometres from the town. The religious part of the festival concludes with the celebration of Mass, but the day continues with picnics, singing and games in the countryside around the Indirizzo area.

On 11th May the feast of Saint Phillip is celebrated. The statue of the Saint is carried out of the church bearing his name in the Casalotto district on the shoulders of young devotees. The crowd greets the arrival of the Saint with firecrackers and cries of "Viva San Fulippu!" (Long live Saint Phillip) and then joins the long procession as it winds through the streets of the old town. At the head of the procession there are donkeys decorated in all colours, used to collect the offerings of the people lining the route.

The feast day dedicated to Our Lady Help of Christians is also popular with local people and sees widespread participation. On 24th May the statue of Our Lady is carried out of the beautiful Church of Saint John in the old town, a church famous for its splendid frescoes by Borremans. This procession also winds its way along the streets of the town, accompanied by the overwhelming perfume of the huge numbers of flowers offered to the Virgin.

Around the end of May the festival of Flowering courtyards and balconies takes place. For a few days the streets, courtyards, balconies and alleyways of Piazza Armerina are richly decorated with flowers, herbs and branches. This ever popular event also includes art and craft exhibitions, as well as other cultural and recreational initiatives.

Every year, from 12th to 14th August, about 500 people on foot and on horseback, dressed in Norman cos-

tumes participate in the Norman Palio, an event unique in its kind in southern Italy.

On 15th August there is a double celebration for the mid-August festival and the celebrations in honour of the Patron Saint. The painting of Our Lady of Victories, patron of Piazza Armeria, is placed on a valuable silver litter, bearing incisions of scenes from the Saint's life, and is carried shoulder high through the streets. The procession leaves the Cathedral in the evening and winds its way around the town to the cry of "Viva Maria!" (Long live Mary), returning to the Cathedral in the small hours.

On the evening of 8th December a mystical procession accompanies the statue of Our Lady of the Immaculate Conception. The crowds are always numerous, even when the winter weather is cold, everyone eager to show their affection for and devotion to Our Lady and to ask for her blessing and protection.

Another important occasion for the people of Piazza Armerina is the feast day dedicated to Saint Lucy, on 13th December. People flock to the Church of Saint Lucy in the Canali district, to show their devotion to this Saint, a virgin and martyr, who sacrificed her eyes rather than renouncing her faith in the Lord. In recent years, at the end of the procession, it has been the custom to offer the participants "cuccìa", a traditional dish composed of boiled corn, served with sweet ricotta or chocolate.

The most important Christmas tradition in Piazza Armerina is the preparation of the "novenas".

Soon after the feast of Saint Lucy, you will see people decorating icons in the streets of the old town with orange branches. In the evening for nine days before Christmas (hence, "novena"), firecrackers are let off and a band plays traditional music in front of each of the "novena", while people pay homage to Baby Jesus.

Gina Gulisano

The Norman Palio

The Norman Palio is a unique spectacle in southern Italy, a festival recreating historical events of a thousand years ago. The Palio is history, because the characters represented are people who really existed, and at the same time legend, since there is no direct evidence that Piazza Armerina was the scene of the events that are recreated.

Count Roger, the youngest son of the Norman King Tancredi, arrived in Italy in the first few years of the millennium in support of his brother Robert, called the Guiscardo, who was engaged in the conquest of Calabria and Sicily, then ruled by the Byzantines and the Saracens.

This conquest was supported by the Church of Rome, indeed Pope Nicholas II, during the Council of Melfi, agreed to grant the Island to the Normans if they succeeded in conquering it and liberating it from Saracen rule.

When the conquest was complete the Pope offered Roger a standard portraying Our Lady with Child; Roger donated the standard to the town of Piazza Armerina as a sign of devotion and thanks to the townspeople, so that it could be venerated on the main altar of the Cathedral. This is the inspiration for the Palio.

In the years following the Second World War ideas were put forward for creating events that would make Piazza a tourist attraction.

Two illustrious citizens of the town, Angelo Urzì and Vito Romano, with the help of willing volunteers, decided to realise a long-standing dream of theirs: to create an event, unique in its kind, symbolically evoking the liberation of Sicily, and in particular of Piazza, from the Saracens by the

troops of Count Roger of Altavilla. Their dream was fulfilled. The first festival was held in 1952 and was such a great success that it was decided to repeat it in following years. It still takes place today, every year from 12th to 14th August.

On the first day the Grand Magistrate parades through the town carrying a lighted lamp, which he then places in the Cathedral in front of the Standard of Our Lady of Victories, as a sign of gratitude and devotion to the Patron Saint. Immediately afterwards the knights from the various districts of the town are blessed before

competing in a jousting tournament, simulating the battle against the hated Saracens.

On the afternoon of the 13th young knights, noblemen and women parade around their own district, along the tortuous winding basalt paved streets of the old town, lined with crowds of people, until they reach the place

where they will pay homage to Count Roger and his troops.

The participants represent the historic districts of Piazza Armerina: Monte, Casalotto, Canali and Castellina. All the parades head for the same destination: the Cathedral square. Here, surrounded by the colourful crowds, they take their places. In the bak-

ing hot sun, they all wait for the crucial moment.

Suddenly, in the distance, you hear the beating of drums carried on the wind and a fanfare of trumpets announces the approach of Count Roger's troops.

Foot soldiers, archers and crossbowmen precede the main body of the army, made up of cavalry.

The arrival of the Count is thus announced by the rhythmic sound of hooves on the road surface.

He is accompanied by pages and equerries and, after dismounting, heads towards the local dignitaries.

From the opposite side of the square, the Grand Magistrate of the town and the Grand Dame, preceded by the Town Crier, come across to meet him.

Next to the bell tower of the Cathedral the Town Crier reads the proclamation: everyone listens in silence.

This first phase ends with a large meaningful bow.

Immediately afterwards the citizens of Piazza swear loyalty to the Norman Count and, to demonstrate the strength of their convictions, present him with the keys to the town.

At this point the parade is reformed and everybody, with Count Roger, the Grand Magistrate and his wife at the head, moves off in a proces-

sion that takes them along the main streets of the town, accompanied by the rhythmic sound of drums and trumpets.

The following day, at the S. Ippolito sports-ground, the knights representing the four districts of Piazza Armerina participate in the so-called "quintana", the most colourful part of the whole three day event.

The knights challenge one another in tests of skill and ability, being awarded points on the basis of their performance. Naturally, the team with the highest number of points wins.

The public watch these competitions with great enthusiasm, everyone giving vocal support to their district. The prize for the knights of the winning team is the famous standard portraying Our Lady of Victories, which is kept in the parish church of the victorious district for a year, until the next competition.

Gina Gulisano

Piazza Armerina Cuisine

The cuisine of Piazza Armerina is based primarily on genuine natural ingredients, enhanced by flavours and herbs used in exactly the right measure: garlic, oregano and basil lend a particular flavour to even the simplest dishes and sauces.

Meat and fish, often barbecued, form the backbone of the local cuisine. The traditional cuisine of Piazza is that of the Sicilian countryside, a cuisine that succeeds in transforming cheap and simple ingredients into delicious tasty dishes.

The ingredients are those grown locally, including unique vegetables that grow wild in the countryside, and so the local diet is a seasonal one, following the natural rhythms of nature.

The cakes are something else altogether since those made locally, and more generally in Sicily, are rich and elaborate, as can be seen from the basic ingredients used: almonds, pistachio nuts, candied fruit, raisins and ricotta cream, a list to make your mouth water.

The recipes below are just a few examples of traditional cuisine, adapted according to the imagination and skill of expert local chefs.

PUMPKIN AND STOCKFISH DUMPLINGS IN CREAMED BROCCOLI SAUCE WITH CLAMS AND BLACK OLIVES

Ingredients:
400g of pumpkin pulp;
200g of fine flour;
150g of desalted stockfish;
10g of shallot;
1 whole egg;
clams;
1/2 glass of white wine;
black olives;

6 anchovy fillets;
extra virgin olive oil;
1 clove of garlic.

Soften the pumpkin in the oven until it is cooked and then sift it into a
bowl. Add the flour, the shallot, the stockfish and a whole egg. Mix together until you obtain a soft mixture.
Put the mixture into a cloth icing bag and squeeze out small lumps
about 5cm in size, letting them fall into a saucepan of boiling water.
As soon as they float take them out and put them into a pan in which you
have sautéed the clams, capers and black olives in extra virgin olive oil,
adding 1/2 glass of white wine at the end.
Cook the Calabrese broccoli in unsalted water and then place them in
a pan with the 6 anchovy fillets, which have already been sautéed with
olive oil and a clove of garlic (which should then be removed).

Chef Angelo Treno from the restaurant "Al Fogher"

PAPPARDELLE "ALLA CENTRALE"
200g of green broccoli;
two kitchen spoons of tomato sauce;
90g of fresh pappardelle;
a glass of olive oil;
1 clove of garlic;
spicy chilli pepper;
basil;
mint;
salted ricotta.

Cook the cleaned and washed broccoli in plenty of salted water.
Fry a mixture of garlic, basil and chilli pepper and add the broccoli after

127

cutting them into small pieces.

Add the tomato sauce and mix together. Cook the pappardelle 'al dente', drain and sauté in the pan.

Serve on a warm plate and with grated salted ricotta and decorated with basil and mint leaves.

"Bocca di lupo" (Wolf's mouth)
80g of very thin veal steak;
a slice of fried aubergine;
a slice of cooked ham without preservatives;
20g of fresh mozzarella;
a glass of dry white wine;
a kitchen spoon of tomato sauce;
a teaspoon of Sicilian pesto;

Slice the aubergines, cover them in salt and place them in a colander for about an hour, until they lose their excess water.

Lay out the veal steak, remove any fat and then place a slice of cooked ham on top of it, followed by a slice of fried aubergine and then the mozzarella.

Fold over the steak carefully so that none of the contents come out.

Brown the steak (bocca di lupo) in a pan greased with olive oil, then singe it with white wine until it evaporates.

Garnish with tomato sauce and mozzarella, then put into a hot oven for about three minutes.

Serve on a platter, adding a teaspoon of Sicilian pesto.

Chef Giuseppe Raffaele from the restaurant "Totò"

RABBIT "ALLA STEMPERATA"

1 rabbit weighing about 1.2kg;
1 onion;
2 sticks of celery;
5 cloves of garlic;
1 spoonful of salted capers;
10 or 12 green olives;
100g of extra virgin olive oil;
sale as required;
a pinch of chilli pepper;
200g of chopped tomato or 2 ripe tomatoes;
4 spoonfuls of white vinegar.

Place the onion, celery, garlic, capers, olives and oil in a pan and fry them.
Wash the rabbit, cut into pieces and add along with salt and chilli pepper; let the rabbit dry and then add four spoonfuls of white vinegar and let it evaporate.
Add the tomato and enough water to half cover the rabbit. Put on the lid and cook slowly for about an hour (it should remain a little soft).

Pioni Fiorella from the trattoria "La Ruota"

Morgantina

This was an architecturally beautiful city and one of great historical importance in the events of ancient history in Sicily.

Morgantina is situated in the heart of Sicily at a point where the mountainous interior begins to slope down eastwards into the Gornalunga valley, towards the vast plain of Catania and the Ionian coast.

The site on which the city stood was, therefore, of great strategic importance, so much so that it was already inhabited in prehistoric times (early bronze age).

In addition to its strategic importance, it was also a zone with a very good water supply and fertile land, unlike most of the arid countryside of the Sicilian interior.

Morgantina is one of the most famous ancient cities in Sicily thanks to being mentioned in numerous ancient works of history and especially because, since 1955, it has been the object of several American archaeological expeditions, in co-operation with the authorities that have been responsible for the site over the years (Siracusa, Agrigento and Enna).

On the hills of Serra Orlando, in other words the same site as the city of Morgantina, there is evidence of the an iron age settlement (early 1st millennium BC), when the Morgeti, a population of Italic origin, came to Sicily with the Ausones and the Sikels, occupying this part of the Island and creating a principality.

The Morgeti brought with them their peninsular culture and tradition, especially the production of metal objects (in iron and bronze) and of characteristic pottery.

The traces of this early phase of the city's existence are composed of huts found under the remains of later buildings, particularly in the area known as the Citadel.

The city was quickly Hellenised under the cultural, political and economic influence of the nearby powerful city of Syracuse. Consequently, Morgantina is one of the best examples of Hellenised native cities in the whole of Sicily.

The achievements of the city, especially from an urban point of view, also make it a unique example of harmony between town planning and environmental concern.

More precise information about the city is available from the era of Ducetius (459BC), the famous King of Sikels, who conquered the city. At the end of the same century Morgantina fell under the domination of Camarina, a colony of Syracuse on the southern coast of Sicily, on payment of a considerable sum of money to Syracuse. However, in the early 4th century BC, Dionysius of Syracuse conquered it in 392 and occupied it for a few years, because the

Carthaginian General Mago succeeded in making the city an ally against Syracuse.

After falling under Roman rule, Morgantina tried to rebel during the Second Punic War but was severely punished for this after being re-conquered and was given to a group of Spanish auxiliaries in 211BC.

From then on the city fell into a rapid decline. It returned to prominence due to an important event in Roman history in Sicily: the slave revolt. It was besieged by Salvio's slaves during the second slave war (104-100BC).

By the advent of the Imperial period the site of the city was practically abandoned.

So ended the story of one of the most important non-Greek cities in Sicily.

Bottom: the Greek Theatre in Morgantina.

THE ARCHAEOLOGICAL AREA

The site of the city was used as agricultural land for centuries.

It is only recently, thanks to the American archaeological mission, that the city has been restored as a place of study and archaeological interest.

You can begin your visit to the ruins at the Citadel since it is the site of the first settlement (founded

around the beginning of the 2nd millennium BC).

This place was chosen by the first settlers, the Morgeti, because it was the highest point and thus the most easily defended.

The town was composed of huts and was well fortified, in a similar way to numerous other native and Hellenised sites found all over the interior of Sicily.

In the archaic period, Greek settlers came to live on the ruins of the previous town, building a sort of acropolis with temples and private houses.

Around the end of the 6th century BC a fort was con-

Bottom: three-sided stairway used for assemblies.

structed, perhaps in reaction to the expansion of Gela and Syracuse, but it was quickly destroyed.

After a long period of abandonment the Citadel was refortified around the middle of the 3rd century BC.

The area with most monuments is the agora, the heart of classical and Hellenistic cities, situated in a valley with a slight slope to the southeast and bordered by gentle hillsides.

The slope would not allow the area to be used practically, so it was eliminated by levelling off and creating two adjacent flat areas on different levels.

The problem for the planners of Morgantina was how to connect the two levels.

This problem was solved in an effective and original way, both from a practical and from an aesthetic point of view. A mighty three-sided stairway

Bottom: circular enclosure of the Sanctuary of the Chthonic gods.

was built, with 15 steps, which, apart from being surprisingly visually effective, was also used for assemblies (ekklesiasterion) or as a place of worship in connection with the sanctuary below, dedicated to the chthonic gods (that is, characterised by a strong link among the endogenous forces of nature).

This was built between the late 4th and early 3rd centuries BC.

The sanctuary had a trapezoidal form and was surrounded by a temenos perimeter wall. It housed several altars and a small sacred chamber divided into a cella and an adytum.

Top:
"Bouleuterion"
area.

The construction of the theatre in the south-western corner of the lower agora dates from the same period. It overlooked the agora and offered a magnificent view over the hills of the Sicilian interior and the upper Gornalunga valley. Unlike most of the other Greek theatres in Sicily, it was not dug out of the rock or laid out on a natural embankment, but rather was built almost entirely in elevation, in a similar way to the much larger theatre at Segesta. The auditorium rested, therefore, on a huge artificial embankment, held in place by a solid quadrangular wall (in Segesta the wall was semicircular) with interior buttresses.

The 14 or 15 levels of the auditorium were divided into six sectors, but there was probably a wooden structure with more rows of seating further back. The total capacity was probably about 5,000 people.

On the eastern side of the lower agora there is a long building with adjacent rooms of varying sizes.

The longer rooms have interior buttresses that were probably used for attaching wooden structures for the storage of grain.

For this reason, this building has been identified as the public granary of Morgantina, which, according to the Lex Hieronica mentioned by Cicerone, was used for storing the grain quotas to be paid to the state.

Top: the Theatre
and Chthonic
Sanctuary.

Fountain with two basins.

The highest part of the agora is of a trapezoidal shape, surrounded on three sides by long narrow covered stoai (wide porticoes supported by pillars). In the northern stoa the end wall was occupied by a series of public buildings, including the prytaneum and the gymnasium.

In the northern corner of the agora, on the long side north-eastern side, there was a large quadrangular fountain with two basins. It was fed by a nearby spring and served both as a decorative feature and as a convenient place for people to collect water.

In the western corner of the area bordered by the stoai, there is a rectangular building with a courtyard leading into a large room. In this room there is a semicircular foundation, followed by a rectangular one, leading experts to believe that this was the bouleuterion, the meeting place for the city assembly, a kind of senate. In the second century BC the building ceased to be used for this purpose and became a thermopolium, a sort of bar.

In the centre of the area surrounded by the stoai is the macellum, a covered market similar to those found in Pompeii, Pozzuoli etc, with a central

The "macellum" with Etna in the background.

circular structure called a tholos, a large courtyard surrounded by a portico on all four sides. On the other side of the portico, there are openings in the walls which housed the various shops.

The hillsides to the east and west of the agora were home to the wealthy inhabitants of Morgantina. The houses were in the same style as those found in other Hellenistic towns in Sicily in the same period. One of the most impressive residences is the so-called "House with the Doric capital", a typical peristyle type house, that is with rooms opening onto a central courtyard with portico.

Some of the rooms had mosaic or earthenware floors. This was a very fashionable type of flooring in the Hellenistic-Roman period, among the wealthy and powerful. By using these techniques, artisans were able to produce very complex decorative patterns, inspired by geometry or by the natural world. The examples in Morgantina include very effective geometric patterns, but there are also early exam-

The "Gimnasium".

ples of mosaics that would come into their full glory during the Imperial Roman period.

The houses have been named according to things found in them or on the basis of the probable owner. Thus, apart from the "House with Doric capital", we have the house of Ganymede to the east of the agora, and those called the houses of the Arched Watertank, of the Antefixes, of the Gold Coins, of the Tuscan Capitals and of the Magistrate, to the west of the agora; these names clearly refer to the structure and decorations of the houses, demonstrating the status of the owners.

These houses were inhabited around the 3rd century BC and were abandoned no later than the 1st century BC, after being sacked in 211 BC.

The whole agora complex was created between the late 4th and early 3rd century BC, when the city moved from the Citadel and began to take advan-

The trapezoidal stairway of the Agora.

tage of the depression in the Serra Orlando plain.

The agora was the most important part of the city. It is an element in the overall city plan, characterised by two or three main roads in a southwest/north-east direction.

The entire agora has a clearly defined public

function. It was designed to host public, cultural and entertainment events for the citizens of Morgantina.

The agora continued to exist in Roman times but it took on a completely different character from the political, cultural and economic centre it had been in the Greek era.

The Romans slowly but surely changed the geopolitical character of Sicily, making it one of

the most important and profitable provinces of the Empire. Many Sicilian cities disappeared for ever and were forgotten, until the archaeologists' spades uncovered their ancient splendour. Other cities continued to exist, losing their previous independence and prosperity.

The floors of the rooms were covered with attractive mosaics or terracotta with geometrical or naturalistic motifs.

Others were created, but these were few and were linked exclusively to the economic growth created by the important communication routes with Africa, such as in the case of Lilibeum.

The political and economic balance also changed in Morgantina.

The city, with its markets and institutions, was no longer the beating heart of the region.

In fact, there was no more need for institutions, since all decisions were taken in Rome, and the local officials were no more than servants of the central authority.

There was no debate and local assemblies served no useful purpose.

A good example of this institutional decline is that of the bouleuterion, which became a bar (thermopolium) in Roman times!

Even the market was now superfluous.

Free trade no longer had the same importance and value it had once possessed for the Sicilian economy.

Now, most of the Island's agricultural produce was destined for Rome, thanks to the system of granting huge estates to veterans or high ranking members of the Roman "nomenclature".

The old market in the agora could only attract purchasers for those few limited items of produce that

House with Doric Capital.

did not fall under the Roman landowning monopoly.

The landowner's estate, therefore, became the seat of real political and economic power.

The wealthy landowner took on the role of a sort of patriarch within the territory under his control.

The villa, rather than the city, was now the political and economic centre of Sicilian life throughout the Roman era and beyond.

The villa of Casale at Piazza Armerina, in whose territory Morgantina was situated, was just one of many that were built in Sicily, but it is certainly the one which gives us some idea today of the luxury and wealth in which these landowners lived, as demonstrated by its elaborate floor mosaics.

Kiln for the firing of pottery.

The collection of mosaics that decorated the floors of the large villa has been described as the most important and most complete ever discovered.

The villa certainly represents the apotheosis of centuries of unchallenged domination, built as it was at the end of the Empire, in the 4th century AD.

This domination by the Romans succeeded in draining the resources of the Island in a way no other conqueror ever managed to equal.

The agora of Morgantina continued to exist into the 1st century BC, until it was sacked in 211 BC.

After it was abandoned, the ruins of the monuments and the private residences were slowly covered by sediments and became agricultural land for centuries, until archaeological digs began and it became an attraction for researchers and tourists.

A kiln.

Sebastiano Tusa

Where to stay in Piazza Armerina

HOTELS

- Park Hotel Paradiso ♥♥♥: contrada Ramaldo. Restaurant, fitness centre, car park and air conditioning (tel.0935/680841 - fax 0935/683391).
- Hotel Villa Romana ♥♥♥: Piazza Alcide De Gasperi. Right in the centre.
  Restaurant, car park and air conditioning (tel.0935/682911 - fax 0935/682912).
- Hotel Mosaici ♥♥: contrada Paratore Casale, 11. In the countryside near the archaeological site. With restaurant, bar and car park (tel. 0935/686054 fax 0935/685453).
- Ostello Del Borgo ♥: largo S.Giovanni 6. Right in the centre. Ex-Benedictine monastery with adjacent church.
  The rooms are the former cells used by the Benedictine monks. (tel. 0935/687019 - fax 0935/686943) www.ostellodelborgo.it e-mail info@ostellodelborgo.it.

BED & BREAKFAST

- Casa Mia Sicilian Quality ♥♥♥: via Chiarandà, 14. Right in the centre. (tel.0935/88088 fax 0935/87941 mobile 338/8720014) www.hotelmorgantina.it/piazza_armerina_ita.htm e-mail hotelmorgantina@tiscali.it.
- Green Valley ♥♥: contrada Leano. In the hills, surrounded by olive groves and vineyards.
  Five kilometres from Piazza Armerina on the provincial road connecting Piazza Armerina with Mirabella Imbaccari. Restaurant service available (tel.0935/89100 mobile 338/1730903).

FARM HOLIDAYS

- Agricasale ♥♥♥♥: contrada Ciavarini. Thirty hectares of unspoilt Mediterranean scrub, four minutes from the town centre. Excellent service. Typical cuisine using natural ingredients, horse-riding, swimming-pool, tennis, 5-a-side football, camper service and campsite.
  www.agricasale.it agricasale@interfree.it (tel./fax 0935/686034).
- Savoca ♥♥♥♥: contrada Polleri (tel.0935/683078). 3.5 km from Piazza Armerina, surrounded by a poplar wood.
  Bus connections to Piazza Armerina and Mirabella Imbaccari. Leisure activities include horse-riding, swimming-pool with sulphurous water, archery, bowls. Typical cuisine using natural ingredients.

- Grottacalda ♥♥♥: contrada Grottacalda. Relaxing environment in a woodland setting. Facilities include stables and playground. Home cooking (tel./fax 0935/958533).
- Il Glicine: contrada Vallegrande (tel.0935/684119 mobile 368/3213006).
- Rural Tourism La Briscola: contrada Bosco – Monte Carubbo - Mirabella Imbaccari (Ct). Restaurant with typical Sicilian cuisine. Archery range, horse-riding, mountain biking and children's playground (tel./fax 0933/991611 – mobile 329/6949723).

WHERE TO EAT

- Al Fogher: two kilometres from Piazza Armerina on the S.S.117 bis road. The chef recommends the pumpkin and stockfish dumplings with black olives, capers and clams, served on a bed of broccoli and the baked breaded scabbard fish with prawns (tel.0935/684123).
- Al Giardinetto: via Lo Giudice, 41. Pappardelle "alla Giardinetto" and breaded cutlet "alla siciliana". In summer you can eat outside with a lovely view over the town centre (tel.0935/682222).
- Al Ritrovo: contrada Bellia on the S.S. 117 bis road. Country style starters, try the strozzapreti with Sicilian pesto and toasted almonds and the mixed barbecued grill (tel.0935/681890).
- Al Teatro: via del Teatro, 6. Restaurant and pizzeria. Try the tagliatelle "alla norma" (tel.0935/85662).
- Bellia: S.S.117 bis road. Excellent pennette "alla boscaiola" and risotto with asparagus tips (tel.0935/680622).
- Da Battiato: contrada Paratore Casale, 11. Restaurant of the Hotel Mosaici. Tagliatelle in sardine sauce, mixed grill, country style salad and almond pastries (tel. 0935/686054 fax 0935/685453).

- Da Totò Centrale: via Mazzini, 29. Restaurant and pizzeria. We recommend the pappardelle "alla Centrale" with vegetables and the baked "bocca di lupo", a steak filled with aubergines, ham and mozzarella (tel./fax 0935/680153).
- Imperial: contrada Casale. Bar and restaurant situated by the entrance to the Roman Villa of Casale. The chef recommends the pasta "alla norma" and the Imperial salad (tel./fax 0935/85750).
- L'Antica Stazione: S.S.117 bis road contrada Ronza. Restaurant and pizzeria (tel. 0935/89220).
- La Capricciosa: via Gen. Ciancio, 38. Restaurant and pizzeria. The rabbit "alla cacciatore" is highly recommended (tel. 0935/682193).
- La Coccinella: via Renato Guttuso, 2. Restaurant and pizzeria. Typical Sicilian cuisine. Wide choice of wines (tel. 0935/682374).
- Papillon: via Manzoni, 60. Restaurant and pizzeria. First courses include cavati "alla Turiddu" and "zite" with herbs (tel. 0935/685524).
- Park Hotel Paradiso: contrada Ramaldo. Typical Sicilian cuisine (tel. 0935/680841 fax 0935/683391).
- Pepito: via Roma, 140. Restaurant adjacent to the municipal park. Typical Sicilian and international cuisine. Paella is available on request (tel. 0935/685737).
- La Ruota: contrada Casale. Trattoria near the Roman Villa. Specialities include: rabbit "alla stemperata" and aubergine "caponata", fresh pasta with wild fennel (tel. 0935/680542).
- La Tavernetta: via Cavour, 14. Trattoria in the town centre. Fish based cuisine. Try the fresh pasta "alla tavernara" with vegetables (tel. 0935/685883).

Bottom: in Piazza Armerina... even cats lick their lips.

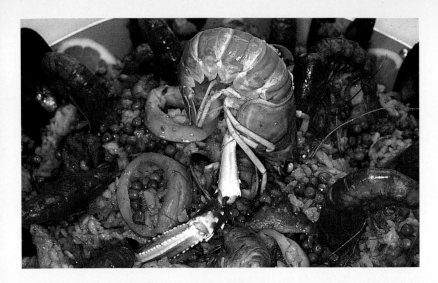

- Sombrero: via Gebbia, 12. Restaurant and pizzeria with wood burning oven (tel.0935/681400).
- Trattoria del Goloso: via Garao, 4.
  we suggest the maccheroncini "alla siciliana" and the roast lamb (tel.0935/685693).
- Villa Romana: Piazza Alcide De Gasperi.
  Local and international cuisine. Tagliatelle "alla romana" and pork roulades "all'ennese" (tel.0935/682911 fax 0935/682912).

Where to stay in Morgantina

HOTELS
- Hotel Morgantina ♥ ♥ ♥: via Adelasia, 42 - Aidon
  (tel. 0935/88088 - fax 0935/87941 – mobile338/8720014).
  Restaurant and pizzeria.
  www.hotelmargantina.it/piazza_armerina_ita.htm
  e-mail hotelmorgantina@tiscali.it

WHERE TO EAT
- Al Cordoba: piazza Cordoba, 5 - Aidone (tel. 0935/88112).
- La Torre: via D. Minolfi, 50 - Aidone (tel. 0935/88088).
  Restaurant and pizzeria. Home cooking.
  www.hotelmorgantina.it
  e-mail hotelmorgantina@tiscalinet.it

LAYOUT OF THE ROMAN VILLA

1 Praefurnia – Ovens for heating the water and air of the spa complex
2/A Male Calidarium; 2/B Sauna; 2/C Female Calidarium
3 Tepidarium
3/A Room for greasing and massage after bathing.
4 Frigidarium – Seascapes in the centre and bathing scenes in some of the niches
5 Large latrine
6 Shrine of Venus
6/A Spa Vestibule for servants
7 Polygonal courtyard with Ionic columns
8 Ancient entrance to the Villa, originally with 3 arches
9 Adventus Vestibule – Guests were greeted in this room
10 Peristyle – Rectangular four-sided portico with 32 columns
10/A Garden containing large pond with statue of Cupid
11 Votive shrine for worship of the Lares who protected Roman households
12 Courtyard
13 Latrine with mosaics depicting running wild animals
14 Large gymnasium – The mosaics depict chariot races in the Circus Maximus
15 Trapezoidal Vestibule – The mosaics probably depict Eutropia, Maximianus' wife and mistress of the Villa, with her children
16 Arab or Norman furnace room
17 Servants' room with geometrical mosaics
17/A Kitchen with basin
18 Room with star patterned mosaic
19 Rectangular room without mosaics
20 Bedroom with dance or theatre inspired decorations
21 Four seasons room
22 Fishing cupids room
23 Small Hunting Room – Hunters making a sacrifice to Diana
24 Servants' room with octagonal patterned mosaic
25 Servants' bedroom. Square patterned mosaics
26 Large Hunting Ambulacrum or corridor (60 metres long)
26/A On the left: apse with mosaics depicting Mauritania (Africa)
26/B On the right: apse with mosaics showing scenes from India or Armenia
27 Servants' room with geometrical patterned mosaic
28 Room depicting ten girls in "bikinis" doing gymnastics
29 Diaeta of Orpheus – Rectangular room for listening to music
30 Xystus – Wide open-air atrium in an ellipsoid shape
30/A Triclinium kitchen
30/B Corridor linking the four-sided portico with the Xystus
31 Putti pressing grapes; 32 Cupids harvesting grapes; 33 Vine growing; 34 Cupids fishing; 35 Eroti fishing; 36 Seafaring putti
37 Triclinium – Large dining-hall with apses on three sides
38 Secondary aqueduct
39 Castellum Aquae (water collection tank)
40 Octagonal latrine for members of the family
41 Diaeta of Arion – The mistress's sitting-room
41/A Atrium with semicircular portico with Ionic columns and central impluvium
42 Vestibule of the small circus – mosaics of chariots driven by children
43 Bedroom (cubicle) used by the mistress's daughter
44 Vestibule of Eros and Pan – The mosaic shows Eros and Pan wrestling
45 Bedroom used by one of the children of the owner of the Villa. In the ante-room mosaics with children hunting
46 Basilica – Large hall for official functions
47 Vestibule of Polyphemus – Large mosaic portraying Ulysses and Polyphemus
48 Fruit cubicle – Bedroom used by the mistress (domina) of the Villa. The mosaics in the ante-room depict laurel wreaths with fruit
49 Bedroom used by the owner of the Villa. Mosaic with erotic scenes